How Did 'The Stock Exchange' Begin?
Rishe Deitsch

It was in the 1980s. I was in my early 20s and working for the *N'shei Chabad Newsletter (NCN)*.

We (*NCN* editor-in-chief Rivki Geisinsky and I) wanted writers who were exceptionally kind or exceptionally wise to write for us. We also liked exceptionally funny. Shimshon Stock fit all three categories, and, with his wife Martha's help and support, he agreed to write. Before each issue, he would hand me many pages filled with his unmistakable long, dark scrawl (which cannot be described —you have to see it).

Rivki named our new column The Stock Exchange.

Why did I feel the Stocks had to write? Because as a teenager I loved hanging out at their house. I knew what they believed not from long lectures, but simply from seeing how they lived and what they did, quietly, for others. And those beliefs had to be put down on paper and spread as far as possible.

After I would receive the handwritten article, I would type and then edit The Stock Exchange, and then I would snail-mail it to Shimshon and Martha for their approval or edits. Yes, snail-mail. This was before email and before fax, and walking through Crown Heights from Schenectady Avenue to Brooklyn Avenue wasn't safe at the time (which is why Shimshon would always put on his coat and walk me home, even late at night, whenever I would leave their house as a teenager).

So I would mail the article and a few days later, I would call for edits. Shimshon hardly had any corrections. He generally approved. However, one time after I had mailed him an edited article to check, he said I should come over. I came over and both he and Martha told me that while they still believed that many people were getting divorced for petty reasons and they should work harder to save their marriages, they also had come to the realization that sometimes divorce was called for and should be supported. "Don't make it so black and white," they said. Very few things in life are totally black and white, they were gently teaching me.

As I left that day, Martha said to me, "Rishe, you are Shimshon's amanuensis." I had no idea what that word meant (I had to go home, take out the physical dictionary, and look it up), but she smiled while she said it so I didn't worry.

Shimshon and Martha Stock and their three children, Benjy, Chanie (Perelmuter), and Faige (Moskovits), lived simply in a small apartment on Montgomery Street, but they gave big to people in any kind of need.

Time, money, a *shidduch*, friendship, a place to date, a home-catered wedding, a late-night walk home... they gave it all. But first they gave food. You ate first, talked later. When someone would walk in with a problem, first they would feed that person a hot meal in a congenial atmosphere, with a few laughs thrown in. After that, the problem always seemed lighter.

I will never forget Thursday nights at the Stock home in the 1970s, with Benjy loading boxes of food and dropping them off at homes late into the night. As the job grew, he acquired some helpers, but he seemed to move the fastest and to carry the heaviest boxes. He worked efficiently, but most of all he had a sense of urgency. You didn't want to

get in Benjy's way on a Thursday night. This is how Chevra Simchas Shabbos v'Yom Tov (CSSY) was born.

In 1977, the Rebbe officially established CSSY as a Chabad organization. After that, Shimshon would walk around 770 collecting money for it, famously calling out: "Take out a dollar and give me the rest!" (Visit cssy.org/about, for more.)

Now CSSY is more sophisticated, but it's still first and foremost about feeding people.

The book you are holding in your hand contains all Shimshon Stock's articles that were published in the *N'shei Chabad Newsletter*.

Shimshon and Martha both passed away in 2007, but their good work continues.

We can still get in on the action by visiting cssy.org/donate. And may all our *yeshuos* come *k'heref ayin*.

I0521863

3

Samples of Reb Shimshon's handwriting

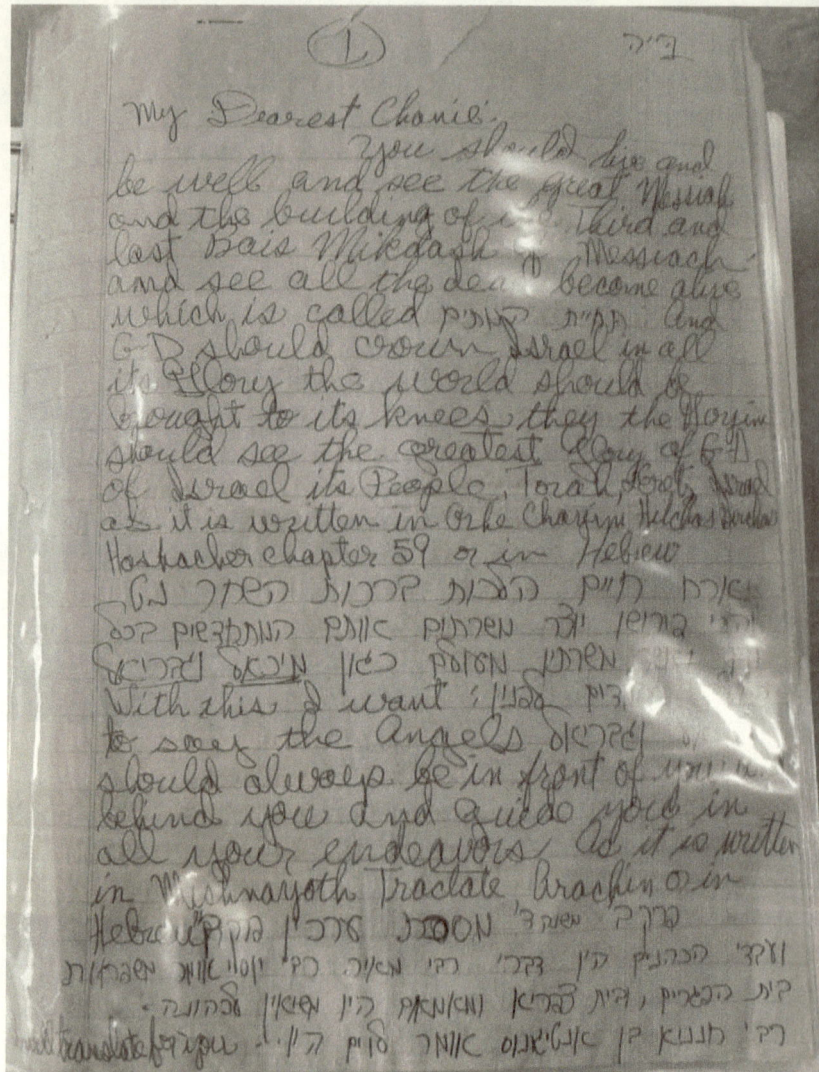

what I have to say about Rashi with
Kadesh the nineteen years is you
Chanie you are going on nineteen
years in my house wondering
and wandering to and fro it is about
time you think of marriage and made
yourself a daughter of a Kohen
into another house preferrable with
a husband and then the angels
ויאמר אראל will watch over both of
you in the greatest time of your
life in holy wedlock or marriage.
NINETEEN YEARS FOREVE) TOTAL 19
LETTERS מות (EVE) TOOK A HUSBAND AN
NOW CHANIE MUST DO THE SAME.

With all my love

שלום בן פ"א מנחם זמן שלום

Table of Contents

Chapter 1 - In Print at Last

Tishrei 5744 – September 1983

I am so happy to be writing many of my thoughts and ideas in the *N'shei Chabad Newsletter* that I don't even know where to begin! There is so much to say! I am drawing on my experiences, having successfully matched up 300 *shidduchim*[1], and thank G-d, most are happy and satisfied people.

What Not to Do

Don't go into a marriage expecting to be showered with gifts, attention, and love. Marry on the basis of give and take. What you give, you will be able to take back. Also, it is not possible to be 100% happy! If you are 50% happy you are doing well. Don't get married because your friends or advisors or even parents advise you that it's a perfect time, perfect person, etc. Marry when and whom you want, not for your friends.

What to Look for

If a friend or a person who you can trust says s/he has a boy for you, ask just two things. Is he a *mentsch*? Is he kind? *Mentschlichkeit* and kindness are the two important things. Ask this question of the one introducing you… not the immediate world! Don't ask everybody else what they think. This is very confusing and 100% unreliable. It is the worst thing to start hearing, "Mm-m I don't think so, you don't look good together, I can't see it. I don't like him, he's too bossy, she's too shy, etc." Why do you need all these opinions before the first date? Form your own opinion!

---

1   Please see the glossary at the back of the book for definitions of this and other Hebrew/Yiddish terms.

Neatness Counts

It is of paramount importance that on the first date both parties should be clean and neat, and the dress or suit should be clean and pressed. I hate to say this, but both parties should shower or bathe before the date, and nobody ever died from a little perfume. In the *Megillah* it says that Queen Esther put on perfume and make-up and looked pretty. And other places in the Torah it is also stated that great women paid attention to their appearance. It is also instructed to a man to marry a woman who is attractive to him, not one who repulses him. By the way, cleanliness, neatness, and attractiveness are important after the wedding also!

My Pet Peeve

If you are not a matchmaker, don't act like one. You can do a lot of harm. Let's say you think A is good for B. So without speaking to B first, you go over to A and say, "I've got a great boy for you!" A gets all excited and happy, but B is not interested when you finally get somebody to speak to him. You have killed a few months of A's dating life, and caused her untold misery, hurt, and rejection. If it were your brother or sister, you would kill the one who made her so unhappy! So, "friends," "advisors," and so-called *shadchanim*, watch what you are doing, and ask yourself, would you do the same to your own child?

A *Shadchan* Must Care

I am very much in love with the kids who come to my house. I have a special feeling for them. Truthfully, their happiness is mine, just to see them married and happy (and out of my house!!). Many Rabbis and *mashpiim* are just not the ones to advise the kids, because they go only according to cold logic. The kids don't need *halachah* and logic; they need as close to a parent's love as possible! From love comes the smartest advice, because if someone loves you they really want the best for you.

Importance of Family

One thing I always insist on is the inclusion of one's parents and family, even if they are not religious. They know what dating and marriage are, don't they? You must get your parents' approval before taking such a big step as getting engaged. I think kids should ask parental advice at all times, *frum* or not. And while dating it is good to discuss it with your parents often. Maybe right now you think they don't understand you, but when you have your own babies you'll crave the closeness of family. Family is important. Don't throw them away now!

Parnassah

I hear that some boys are afraid to come talk me. They say I scream and yell at them. I welcome this opportunity to tell you what makes me scream and yell at them: a man 32 years old who says he is ready to get married, and he is learning and plans to continue learning for another couple of years or so. Living on charity is not a way of life to plan on, *lechatchilah!* G-d forbid if circumstances change and one is forced to turn to charity, that's different—but to plan on it! They get married, and before long there are babies in the house, and then they have to run to Simchas Shabbos V'Yomtov to live. I believe work and Torah keep the family strong. There are plenty of hours in the day for work *and* learning. I tell the boys that if you work from 9 to 5, then spend a few hours with your wife and kids, and then go learn from 8 to 9 at night, and also from 6:30 to 7:30 in the morning, your wife will respect you and so will your kids, G-d will be happy with you, and there will be money for food and clothes and rent.

Don't Wait to Hear Bells Ringing

I want to tell you a little story to end off with. There was once a man who was stuck in his house because the rain was coming and flooding the city. All the people were running for their lives any way they could, but this one man stayed in his house and said, "G-d will help me." A boat passed by his house, and the man in the boat shouted out to him, "Come into my boat, I will save you!" But the man just replied, "G-d will help me." The water got higher, and the man was forced to go to the second floor. As he stood there by the window, another boat went by, and the man in the boat yelled, "Quick! Jump into my boat, before you drown!" But the man still replied in perfect faith, "Don't worry, G-d will help me." Finally the man was forced to stand on the tip of his roof, the flood was so high. A helicopter came by with a ladder hanging down, and the pilot yelled, "Grab hold of the ladder and I'll save you!" But the man replied, "G-d will help me." Suddenly an enormous heavenly voice was heard, saying, "Jerk! I sent you two boats and an airplane. What do you want, an angel with wings?!"

It is the same thing with *shidduchim*. When you go out on a date, don't keep saying, "G-d will send me my *'basherte.'*" Don't keep saying no.

Looking for the Good

When you are meeting a prospective husband or wife, look for the good, not just the faults. It's not necessary to search out every little fault a person has with a magnifying glass. Would you like him or her to do that to you? If you find yourself noticing a lot of faults, look at your own faults; you may suit each other perfectly!

I have a famous mirror in my front room: a full-length one. I usually take a person over for a good head-to-toe look before a date. Just for starts, I say, "Look at yourself before you start criticizing someone else."

Chapter 2 - We Need Each Other

Kislev 5744 – December 1983

Marrying Out of the Fold

I see many young ladies in their late 20s and 30s for whom I can't find Lubavitcher young men. If I can't find them, believe me, they don't exist! Therefore I've been forced to come to the conclusion that we must accept *shidduchim* from out of Lubavitch. I described in the last issue what to look for in a husband— kindness and *mentschlichkeit.* If there is a man who is kind and good and a *mentsch,* is *shomer Shabbos,* and makes a living, then the girl must give the boy a chance even if he is not a Lubavitcher *chossid.* We must be open-minded on this subject. Nobody should talk a girl out of this type of *shidduch!* Boys from other yeshivos come to me, too, and sometimes they are just right for these girls. I am not referring only to B.T.'s, but to lifers as well, although many people are saying that these articles are only for B.T.'s.

It's Good to Be Married

When I used to go to Israel to visit my father for only three weeks while my wife stayed home with our children, it was terribly lonely. There was nobody to visit with, complain to, or fight with. Just to come home to somebody is worth marriage. That's the best reason to get married: to escape loneliness.

Sometimes couples have problems and they think, "I'd be happier alone." It's not true! Don't be deceived by those rosy articles in the women's magazines, entitled, "Single Again and Loving It," or, "Free at Last," or, "The Many Advantages of Living Alone." Those articles on the joys of raising children single-handedly are PURE BALONEY. It's not joyful. It's awful, both for the parent and the children. It is a 100% true fact that no child of divorced parents can remain unaffected and unhurt. This is true whether the child is one week old or 45 years old. It's a terrible pain to inflict on one's children. Of course there are certain very rare cases where divorce is absolutely necessary; for example, when the husband beats his wife. No wife can live with a sicko like that. And there are other good reasons to divorce; I know that. But it kills me to see people divorcing for stupid reasons, like to get even or hurt the other person. This is thinking selfishly, and in the end it's not even good for you; it's just plain lonely. It's very bad that often a divorcing couple doesn't think; they don't think about working it out together or forgetting the fight. If they would only think back to how the fight started they would see how stupid it is. Divorcing as a result of fighting or "incompatibility" is like taking all the food out of the refrigerator and sweeping everything off the cabinet shelves, into the garbage, just because somebody in the house is overweight. Isn't that solution a bit strong?!

Working Things Out for the Greater Good

It's funny; second marriages usually work out well even though the partners may have been previously unsuccessful with other people. Why?

People enter a second marriage with two feet planted solidly on the ground, no heads in the clouds. They are prepared to overlook small offenses for the greater good. I must tell you this story. A woman went to her butcher and asked for only the best chicken. She then began checking it. She searched for a flaw with a magnifying glass—she checked the legs, the wings, the neck, everything. The butcher finally asked her, "Lady, do you think you could pass the same test?"

Trying Hard

Besides overlooking faults, it is also important to work hard in a positive way to make a marriage good. How many couples go out on a date after they are married! Even to look around a museum for two hours? How many times has the husband said to his wife, "Let's go for a ride"? After five years or 25 or 50, it's good for a couple to be alone sometimes and go on a date just to talk and enjoy each other's company. It breaks the monotony of seeing each other every night over the same table, eating the same suppers. It's good just to take a walk in Manhattan or Queens, just to get away from Brooklyn. Or if you live in Queens, go for a walk with your wife in Brooklyn. Seeing each other in a date-like setting brings back the memories of what you saw in each other to begin with: the very reasons you got married. Just think, men, what it would do for your marriage if you brought your wife one rose tonight, or if you complimented her on her new *shaitel*, or better yet, if you offered to put the kids to sleep so she can sit down for a few minutes! Husbands, please try to be good to your wives. If you had to pay someone to do what she does, you couldn't afford it, or even find it. Remember that besides being a mother, your wife is also a woman. (From all the comments I received on Part I of this series, I know for sure that the men read the *N'shei Chabad Newsletter* too. That's why I am addressing these words to the husbands right now.) To help you appreciate your wife, why don't you change places with her for one day? You'll see how hard it is to be wife, mother, teacher, doctor, maid, advisor, cook, companion, friend, chauffeur, doorman, plumber, and general-maintenance "man." You've got all these people in your one wife! I beg you, husbands, just show your wife kindness. Remember her each day with love. Stop off and get that rose. Appreciate her.

Working Mothers

I have nothing against women working, especially when it's a financial help. When my wife worked it was a big help; we were able to afford good tuition in yeshivos and weddings for our children. But a woman shouldn't lose sight of why she's working—for the family and for the children. For their sake, there's nothing more important than being there when the child comes home from school. I feel that a child must find his mother home after school. I already explained in the last issue my very firm belief that a man should do everything in his power to earn a decent living.

Let's Talk

The opinions seen in this series are mine: my personal thoughts and experiences. There have been many different reactions from readers, both men and women. Some people didn't like the picture on top; some laughed, some cried. Others said, "I could hear Shimshon talking." If anybody has a question or anything to say, please, mail it to me at 593 Montgomery Street. You don't even have to sign your name. One time I gave a lecture to young ladies of marriageable age. It caused a lot of heartache and aggravation. People take what I say/write and they run away with themselves. Walk, don't run. Let's talk. Let's think about it and analyze it together. I just want to hear what you think. There's no need for misunderstandings between friends.

In conclusion I want to tell you that there is no time that I will stop doing *shidduchim* as long as G-d gives me strength. To all my dear friends I wish all the best, including good health, happiness in your home, and lots of *nachas* from your children.

Yours,
Shimshon

Chapter 3 - Give to Others

Shvat 5744 – February 1984

We pray on Yom Kippur, "Don't throw me into old age!" And yet, everyone must grow old eventually, and it's not necessarily tragic. What this prayer says is, "Don't let me be alone and lonely." Whether at one day old or at 85 years old, to be alone and uncared for is the most terrible state to be in. And yet, sadly enough, it is prevalent here in our own community. What can we do about it?

A *Shlichus*

You don't have to go to the other side of the world to fulfill the Rebbe's *shlichus*. You can follow the Rebbe's example, and directives, of *ahavas Yisroel*, right here in Crown Heights. What I am encouraging is this: Every person who is settled here in Crown Heights should take it upon himself/herself to give physical and moral support and help to the lonely and problem-ridden couples, children, and especially singles who live around us. OPEN YOUR HOME! OPEN YOUR HEART! You are really needed to help your neighbors.

These Are Our Children!

It doesn't take lots of money or an enormous house; you can help people just by being there, by listening and showing concern for the problems being shared. Do you know how many children under the age of 18 and as young as 12 have been sent here to study in our *mosdos* from out of town, even from across the ocean? Who looks at them, who cares about them? Most members of the *hanhalah* do care but they are very few compared to the number of kids who are here. They live in basements, in apartments, in dorms, or have room and board arrangements with families. They are everywhere. Does anyone ask them if they are happy, if they get enough to eat? If they have a comfortable clean place to sleep? If they get any heat? If school is too hard? If they are keeping in contact with their parents? I know for a fact that there are girls who are ashamed to invite themselves to somebody's house for the Shabbos meals. You meet someone in 770, you hire a babysitter, your daughter's or son's friends, stop admiring their "independence" —it's only skin-deep. Invite them over; show that you really care. Walk them home on Friday nights, even if it's cold outside. *These are our children!*

Not Just Children

I am not only referring to the teenagers. There are many, many singles too, many in their thirties and forties and older, who need good friends to help them adjust to the *frum* life in Crown Heights and make lives for themselves. There are also elderly people who need someone to talk to, a meal, a phone call.

My father, of blessed memory, told me this: "When a little child cries, everybody turns around and tries to help. When an old person cries, it is too often ignored, and that person is just passed over as if it's rain that is falling, and not a lonely person's tears."

If you open up your hearts to these people, young and old, I promise you, G-d will help you that your children will never need to ask for help from strangers.

Humility

Frankly speaking, our problem is that we are sometimes lacking in compassion. If we would sit up straight and come to appreciate the good things that G-d gives us, we would become humble and act kindly towards those who are less fortunate. We don't know how to say, "Thank You, G-d." Relatively good health, a decent spouse, sweet children, and *parnassah* are all basic things that we should appreciate. If you are lacking one of those things, then surely there are other areas in life where you have been blessed. So share, and care. Be grateful.

The True Meaning of FAMILY

I am not a *tzaddik*, but I have realized one thing: This whole world, a lifetime, is but a short dance before the music ends. So don't kill yourself for stupid things, because in the end all that remains is your name and any good work that you did. So let's treat each other like real family, since deep down we are related to one another.

To Start the Ball Rolling

Here are some practical suggestions which are really wonderful ways to start caring for the people around here who need it. Some are easier. Some are harder. Some I didn't write here but you can think of them yourself (and please do!).

Say hello or Good Shabbos to every Jew you meet. Say it with a smile. Get rid of the long faces which don't help anyone at all. Enjoy life. Concentrate on what gives you happiness and satisfaction and you will notice that the people around you are more cheerful now, too. If you know that a family is having a problem, move fast and get to the root of the problem and help solve it. Give a single person advice and practical help in wearing the right clothes, looking good. Help them to go out on dates, even if you have to lend, for an evening, your car or your living room or your money or even your clothes!

We did not buy houses in order to rent our basements to these kids and get rich. We must see to it that they are eating meals, too. Not potato chips and cookies three times a day and Mermelstein's coleslaw for Shabbos! These are our children. Don't forget them.

Sometimes all someone needs is a phone call on their behalf to someone in authority. Do it for them. Maybe you can help people to plan a budget, to make ends meet on a

small salary. When you see a problem, speak up. Don't wait for it to get worse, and hope that it will fix itself. Then you can say, "I saw it coming." You saw it coming? So why didn't you do something? I can give example after example, from some sad personal experiences, but the bottom line is:
LET'S BEGIN!!

Yours truly,
Shimshon

Chapter 4 - Marriage Means Commitment

Pesach 5746 – April 1986

Practice Makes Perfect

The beginning of a marriage is like a new job. It takes about two years to really break in and learn the ropes. It takes time and maturity and sensitivity to accept the fact that each and every person has his or her moods; no one is the same every day, and this holds true especially for newlyweds. Give yourselves time, and be forgiving, and you can probably work things out yourselves, without letting small misunderstandings become major conflicts.

But if you feel you must speak to someone for advice, go to only one person—one very good and close friend. If you really look truthfully, you only have one, maybe two, good close friends. Newlyweds who think they might have a problem they must discuss with a third party should not go for advice to another newlywed couple! Also, never sit with a friend and match problems, compare spouses, etc., because that is betraying a trust. Trust is the basis of a good marriage, and if that's gone you really have problems.

Don't sit around and mope. This goes for any kind of problems, including a marriage-related one.

Money

One of the major problems with young couples is money, and I want to discuss this openly. It upsets me to see young couples on tiny salaries fill their homes with guests. *Hachnasas orchim* is very great but *shalom bayis* is even greater! If you pack your house with guests and therefore fight because there's no money, it's no *mitzvah*. So, these young couples start shopping for their houseful of guests. They have "bills" at the grocery, the butcher, and the fruit store. And don't think it stops there. They need *nosh* for the guests so they now owe the *nosh* store too. They need linen so their guests can sleep over, so they owe the linen store too.

For the sake of *shalom bayis*, don't do this! The first few years take in one or two guests for eating only, two Shabbosos a month. The other two, stay home, just the two of you, and eat by candle-light (saving electricity, too) or eat out at a friend's or relative's house.

Having sleep-in guests adds stress and tension to a newlywed couple's life. What do they need that extra strain for? There will be time for that, later. Try to avoid it in the beginning of your marriage. A relaxed atmosphere is essential in a new marriage in order for closeness and *shalom bayis* to thrive and grow.

It is very beautiful to give *tzedakah* (where would C.S.S.Y. be without it?). But newlywed couples on a tight budget have to realize their limitations. Some young couples have started to give way more than *maaser* to *tzedakah*. They've even given head-checks that eventually bounce!

Every bouncing check costs $10.00. One person told me he gives a lot of *tzedakah* ... but he hadn't paid his rent in three years.

It's also not sensible to spend every penny on gorgeous furniture. What's wrong with the Buy Lines, good used furniture? Who knows what will happen when you move away?

Somebody just told me this story. She went to buy a dress on Kingston Avenue, but decided that $175 was too much for one dress. The next day, she saw that dress on a neighbor's daughter, that neighbor who always borrows money from her for basic necessities and emergencies like the utilities being disconnected. It is important to spend your money and newfound (married) independence with maturity and foresight. Do what is best for *shalom bayis* and also be a *mentsch*.

Don't go into debt as a newlywed, not for guests, not for recliners, and not even for *tzedakah*. Don't be ashamed to look clean and neat, if not up to the minute in style. You sleep better if you live within your means.

Interference

A word to those surrounding a newlywed couple: They are better off with no interference, generally speaking. They need no advice from their friends and parents, they need to work things out by themselves. Close family members should certainly not volunteer to get involved.

I hope no mother-in-law will get offended (remember, Martha is a mother-in-law too).

Pesach

Pesach is almost here. I am speaking to the young couples and the people who are having a hard time financially. Please, when you take guests, take a number that doesn't burden you and your family financially.

A new service of C.S.S.Y. is to help people budget themselves and thus make their financial burdens easier. May G-d give everyone an easy life with good health, opportunities to give lots of *tzedakah* and much *Yiddishe nachas*.

Wishing you the best,
Shimshon

Chapter 5 - Shimshon: Another Dr. Spock?

Kislev 5747 – December 1986

My dear readers and friends, keep in mind that I am not a professional counselor. I can just tell you what I have learned in my over 50 years of life.

It might seem odd or presumptuous of me, Shimshon, to talk to you about raising children. Marriage, yes. Dating, yes. Business, yes. But raising children?

Yes, raising children. I have some experience since I have, *baruch Hashem*, three children, all married now, although I wish G-d had given me more. But thank G-d for these. I'm very proud of them and they're better than nothing.

Also, I have the right to talk about raising children because I do not put myself up as "the expert" —I'm the first to admit that I've made mistakes. I'm just another parent, who tried my best together with a good mother, my wife, Martha.

So here's what I know about raising children.

Three L's: Love, Listen & Learn

The best way to show love and affection to our children is by listening to them, and really hearing what they are saying. Kids are smart and they have opinions, ideas, fears, and hopes, even before they turn three. So start listening early! If you decide when the child turns 15 to start listening he won't have anything to say to you by then. Communication between children and parents must be a habit from babyhood or else it won't happen later on.

When you speak to your good friend, would you say, "Get over here already, would you?" or would you say, "Could you come here for a second please, if you're not busy?" Well, speak to your child with the same decency as you would speak to your friend. You'll get their respect in return.

Children need time for talking with their parents, not just a half-minute on the way out while you put on your *shaitel* or between haircuts at the barbershop. Give your children plenty of time. You find time for the other things you really want to do, don't you? You've found time to read a few books this year, to take a few naps, to yak on the phone for a few hundred hours. So find time for your children, who are your life. Time is so cheap when you're wasting it. But it's so valuable when you are giving it to your child.

By Example: The Only Way

The things you say to your child (or within his hearing) will remain with him forever, and come up later to surprise you. When my father, *a"h*, brought me up I never heard a bad word about a *cheder rebbi* or about anybody, and I never heard that he fooled anybody in business. This attitude of decency toward a fellow Jew remained with me.

When my son Benjy was turning three years old, I went to the Rebbe, *shlita*, and asked him for a *brachah* that Benjy should be a *talmid chacham* and a *chossid*. The Rebbe, may he live and be well, said to me, "*You* show him."

And that's the basic, painful truth, friends. We can't blame the schools. We can't blame the undesirable elements in this neighborhood. We can't blame the president or the mayor or the tenant or the landlord if our child has *chutzpah* or lack of *midos tovos*. We can only blame ourselves, the parents, and the home. The parents are responsible for bringing up their child; ultimately, no one else has that responsibility.

If a child hears *lashon hara* constantly spoken in his house, what kind of adult will he become? Kind and considerate? Or cynical and selfish, G-d forbid?

Don't Be Afraid of a Hug

Of course the basis of good parenting is communication and setting a good example, as explained above. But showing love has another meaning, too, and that is the plain *p'shat*: giving a child a hug, a kiss, a pat once in a while. No one is too old to need that. I just read recently someplace about a woman who broke down at the age of 30 and told how from the time she'd turned 10, she had gone into the bathroom after her mother got dressed, and she had taken the tissue with her mother's lipstick on it out of the wastebasket and held it to her cheek, for comfort. Because as soon as she'd turned 10 her mother had told her, "Now you're too old to kiss."

I don't understand it. There are some women, mothers of children, who are always walking around all dressed up but without their children! Shabbos afternoon or whenever, they're out without the kids, consistently. They have better people to hang around with, or what? Hold your child's hand. Walk proudly with him!

But don't be a good friend to your child. He has plenty of friends at school and on the block, I hope. From you he needs firmness, good strong limits, but also love. That's a parent's job.

If you made a mistake, admit it to your child. He'll love you. A child loves a parent, right or wrong, and a parent must also accept a child, right or wrong. Give your child the gift of truthfulness and he will return the gift to you, and be able to admit his mistakes.

Fulltime Working Mothers

Now I know this is a controversial topic but if you know me, I'm a controversial person. Now I am not condemning the woman who absolutely must work or else live on charity, for example, the single parent. But when mothers leave their kids with other people—it doesn't matter who, it's not their mother—and go off to work all day, coming home exhausted, please don't tell me about your personal fulfillment. What about your kids? The children you gave birth to will suffer now and later if you try to dump them, escape them, or run away from the responsibilities (and the joys). And guess what? Whatever bad treatment you give them, you will have to sit back one day and watch them do these terrible things to your grandchildren and you won't be able to say a word.

Mothers of large families cannot be part-time mothers. Don't let anyone make you feel guilty or "unfulfilled" because you're not working outside the home! If you have the choice, take care of your own children, that's the best job you can do, one that pays off in later years and right away, too.

I beg you, don't run away from your home and children! The home doesn't have to be beautiful and rich. It has to be clean and happy!

May you all have many very happy and healthy years ahead of you, an easy upbringing of your children in the ways of Torah and Chassidus, and much prosperity.

It's a little late to ask forgiveness, but I missed the Tishrei issue of this magazine due to hospitalization so let me say it now: Everybody should please forgive me if I ever hurt them in any way, physical, mental, financial, or with my tongue or pen.

Yours with Love,
Shimshon

Chapter 6 - The Missing Word

Tishrei 5748 – September 1987

One word is missing by us Jews lately that almost makes us, *chas v'shalom* and *l'havdil*, like the *goyim*. It's a word that's supposed to be a special characteristic of Jews: compassion, *rachmanus*. It means that you feel with someone else. When his pain hurts you, that's compassion. There's a special need for compassion right now in this community towards a special segment of the community, and I'd like to speak out on their behalf.

Single, Older Women

As you know I am a small-time *shadchan*, or I try to be when I can. When the girls in a group start getting married, well, somebody has got to go last! And making new friends isn't as easy as it sounds. So a few single, older girls are left behind, forgotten, lonely, and feeling rejected. Who cares for them? These older, single women don't need your dorms. They don't need your jobs. They just need *you*, your friendship, your time, your warmth, your interest, your compassion.

I'm far from a *tzaddik* myself in this area. Sometimes I cross the street not to face them, not to look them in the eye and feel that pain.

I know what I must do, though—and you too. I must cross back over the street and stop them and say hello and be a true friend. These girls need support and encouragement to dress well, look good, take care of their apartments and jobs, and go to lectures, study groups, and social gatherings. They need homes to go to on Shabbos and Yom Tov. They need all of us just to be there for them.

And Others, Too

There are many different people who cannot cope with their present situations. And did you ever find yourself in a desperate situation, truly terrible—then talked it over with someone for five minutes and walked away with the situation unchanged but *you feel better?* Because you talked it out, that's why. What a simple but profound gift to give a person having difficulty coping—a few minutes of attentive, compassionate listening. Or even just a few seconds of silent support, of, "I know this can't be easy for you."

Of course, there are others who need compassion besides single, older women. Here are some ideas but I'm sure that if you put your mind to it you can, unfortunately, double this list.

1) Single mothers and single fathers.

2) Parents of a seriously ill child (it doesn't "get easier to bear" with time—it gets harder).

3) People caring for sick, elderly parents in their homes.

4) Widows, and widowers.

5) People married to drug addicts, alcoholics, the chronically depressed or mentally ill, the unemployed.

6) Parents of large families who need three days away by themselves once a year to restore sanity and regain perspective.

Ask Someone What's Cooking

Let's stop bickering and let's stop talking *lashon hara*. Why don't we just concentrate all that negative energy into compassion, into positive energy, into love?

When I stop a friend and ask, "What's cooking?" I mean it literally. Do you have enough food to cook? A job? The rent money? Your health? There's a catch. Asking someone what's cooking in this way entails a certain responsibility to help out if nothing's in the pot.

I wish people busy with nonsense, with fighting and destroying others, would take an hour off from this important *mishugass* of theirs and visit a mental hospital, or other place where the world's tragedies gather in one room and the pain is sometimes so intense you can't shake it off for a week afterwards. There they would see problems that would perhaps cause them to see others with more compassion, to drop the nonsense and concentrate on their real values, Torah values, G-d, and family.

Mixed Up Parents, Mixed Up Children

And when the majority of parents in this community rethink their values and start acting like they truly should and want to act, then 99% of the problems with our children will disappear too. Children of parents with mixed up values are confused, insecure, defensive and searching. Yes, searching. They've got *"frumkeit,"* you might say— but it's tasteless and empty to them. They're searching for true meaning as much as the kids out there who grew up on Elvis Presley and Kentucky Fried Chicken, *l'havdil.* A television is not a teacher; a parent is the only true teacher. This is why I believe, like many people who have seen the ill effects of doing otherwise, that children should be home with their mothers until they are at least three years old. But I already discussed my views on raising children in my most recent article. If your little babies are still being thrown, kicking and screaming and crying, on the van to the day care center at 18 months old, please reread that article. If they go submissively, but with a sad look in their eyes, it means they're crying inside, but they know it'll do them no good to show their feelings. They have given up.

Find the Missing Word

This article, and I will try to stick to the topic, is about compassion. Let's use the phones to give compassion. Let's use time spent hanging around in front of 770 to give compassion. Let's use every day to give compassion. You don't know how long you will live—if today is your last day, don't you want to use it to be kind, not cruel? And what if today is the needy person's last day—don't you want to be kind to him now, while he can still smile back? Don't come crying to me after someone dies: "I was rotten to him." Just be good to him now. If you were unkind to someone and s/he died, and you're left with a lot of useless, debilitating guilt, let me point something out: There are plenty of people still alive who need your kindness!!

Everything I say to you, my friends, I also say to myself.

I wish everybody good. Blessings to you all for a healthy and prosperous New Year, a year in which we come to understand one another, and learn to live in harmony amongst ourselves.

Peace,
Shimshon

Chapter 7 - What Are We Growing?

Summer 5748 – June 1988

Everybody always nods their heads— "Oh, yes, this certainly is a growing community, with new *baalei teshuvah* coming in every day, and everyone having *ka"h* very large families… we're growing, alright!" My question is, *what* are we growing? Are we growing happy, well adjusted *chassidishe kinder*, or troubled parents and troubled children?

I'm referring to the many singles and young couples completely without families, without parents or relatives who are the least bit interested in them. Those of you who, *baruch Hashem*, have relatives, in-laws, or whatever, you may say at first glance that you're on your own and you receive very little help from your relatives. But when you really think about it, who came through for you when you had that appendicitis attack a couple years ago? Who cleared the tables and wrapped up the food after the last *bris*? Do Bubby and Zaide remember your child's birthday? And crow over a good report card? Think about it and you'll come up with many more good examples yourself.

Well, there are young couples living here without a soul to call upon, ever. Their friends are only other couples like themselves, who also need help. I'm not referring to *mashpia*-type spiritual guidance, no. I'm talking about good old-fashioned family help, the kind most young adults receive from their parents, grandparents, aunts, uncles, and siblings. Our *baalei teshuvah* do not have that entire network of support. It is up to the rest of us to step in as surrogate Bubbies and Zaidies and provide that network of support.

Older People, Here's Your Chance!
There are *baruch Hashem* many older people here in the community whose own children are grown and married, and many of their children have moved away on *shlichus*. Retired from jobs and with some time on their hands, here is the perfect place to invest experience and energy. Adopt a young family who needs you for a shoulder to lean on. Someone to remember the children's birthdays, a supper invitation once a month, a financial gift before Pesach, some advice about work or childrearing or being nicer to one's spouse.

Who can do this work? Who can find Bubbies and Zaidies for all the young couples on their own? If it means going house-to-house, both to ascertain the needy and to recruit the helpers, it must be done.

Shul Shabbos Morning
You, young fathers with children... how do you sleep at night when there's a young widow or divorcee right on your block with small children the same ages as your own children, and you don't offer to take them to shul Shabbos morning with you?

Must she be reminded every day that she is alone with small children to raise or can she sometimes see that she has friends to fall back on?

I once witnessed a terrible scene. A young widow with three small children was waiting for the van to take her kids to school so she could be at work by 9:00. It was snowing and the van didn't show up. The young mother turned to a young man about to go into his car and drive his kids to school: "Would you take my kids to school also?" The man looked at her kids, who had snow on them— "I can't take them. They'll ruin my car upholstery, they're full of snow!" The woman looked sort of lost for a minute.

What was she going to do, when she had to be at work in 15 minutes? But she marshaled her spirits and went in to call a cab, and to call her boss that she would be late. When she came out the man said, "I insist on paying for the taxi, I feel bad that I'm not taking them." She refused to take it of course (how crude to offer it!) and the man had no way of stilling his conscience, his "guilt offering" having been rejected.

Baruch Hashem, now that young woman is happily remarried. She feels grateful to those who helped her in her years of widowhood. And that man, the neighbor with the car, lost his only chance to give her a helping hand in her hard time. His car still looks beautiful. But he can't take the car with him after 120 years.

If there's a single mother on your block, for Heaven's sake, call her up on Thursday and invite her for Shabbos lunch. Say to yourself: There, but for the grace of G-d, go I.

Eleven Years and Waiting

C.S.S.Y. is in operation for almost 11 years already, and I have yet to receive a call from someone asking in whose life they can become productively involved. Believe me, my biggest hope is that C.S.S.Y. should become obsolete and go out of business but if it doesn't, may I please hear from you? If you can't give money, give time. If you can't give time, give money. If you can't give either, maybe we can help you.

In Conclusion

There are three reasons people tell me their problems. Number one: Because I listen. Number two: Because they think maybe I can help. And number three: Because they figure if I can't help at least they can count on my big mouth to get the problem publicized and maybe then they will get some help. So here's a problem people are telling me a lot about lately.

Tenants and Landlords

Tenants have many complaints about their landlords. They never fix anything, they raise the rent, etc. But tenants should look at the other side of the coin too, and ask themselves: Am I doing everything I, as a tenant, am supposed to be doing? Namely, do I take care of the apartment and do I pay my rent on time? You as a tenant may have a thousand good reasons for paying your rent late, but the landlord must pay the mortgage and heating bills and the bank won't listen to excuses. Understand this and don't make your landlord beg every month. It's not fair, it's very uncomfortable, and if you do it anyway then don't scratch your head and wonder why the landlord wants you out.

Tishrei Look-Ahead

By the time the next issue of this *N'shei Chabad Newsletter* comes out it will be already Rosh Hashanah or close to it so I will say this now. Don't overspend. Watch your budget. If you don't have, then don't spend. Debts are not worth it. I wish everyone a healthy, happy summer, one that's easy on the finances, and may G-d give you everything you need, always.

Love,
Shimshon

Chapter 8 - Addressing the Epidemic

Shvat 5749 – February 1989

Yes, I call it an epidemic. Because it's contagious and debilitating. I'm going to say the D-Word now. Divorce. It's everywhere, even here! Rampant! How about you? Have you, too, considered getting a divorce? After all, your husband/wife is not the same person you married, is he/she? Well, think again! There's nothing waiting for you out there after your divorce but pain and regret.

I have seen and heard this so many times, it makes me sick already: A couple is happily married the first few years. Then, people change. They grow up, their interests change, sometimes they go through a hard time and withdraw temporarily from their spouses.

Years ago, in a case like this the spouse gives a *krechts* and waits it out. The waiting spouse knows that the other one will eventually warm up again, if he/she continues to receive warmth and love and support in return.

I'm not saying anyone should swallow unfair treatment and just go to bed. You'll get an ulcer that way. You have the right, the obligation even, to deal with what bothers you... but in a way that says, every second, "This is a problem we will work out. I love you and you love me and we belong together." If that statement is always under their breath, a couple can work through almost any problem, and I have seen some real toughies worked out.

Sneak Preview for Potential Ticket Buyers

Maybe a lot of people jump into divorce after thinking it over for three months because they don't really know what it's like to be divorced. Maybe they picture life continuing on just as comfortably as before, just without that pain-in-the-neck spouse. Well let me give you a sneak preview before you buy a ticket to this tragedy show. Here's what it's really like.

The misery of being divorced can be divided into two categories: the emotional and the physical.

Emotional

Since I'm just a plain simple writer I'm going to let a fancy one say this for me. The following words were written by Pat Conroy in *Atlanta Magazine*. The article is entitled "Death of a Marriage."

Each divorce is the death of a small civilization. Two people declare war on each other, and their screams and tears infect their entire world with the bacilli of their pain. The greatest fury comes from the wound where love once issued forth.

I find it hard to believe how many people now get divorced, how many submit to such extraordinary pain. For there are no clean divorces. Divorces should be conducted in abattoirs or surgical wards...

Divorce should be declared a form of insanity, or a communicable disease (how often married couples seem to feel threatened around their divorced friends). I have seen no one walk out of a divorce unmarked; it makes you a different person. You can enter the sinister cocoon as a butterfly and stagger out later as a caterpillar doomed to walk under the eye of a spider... There are no laws of nature that apply— only laws of suffering different for each individual...

[Divorce is] a country, and it is treeless, airless; there are no furloughs and no holidays. One enters without passport, without directions and absolutely alone. Insanity and hopelessness grow in that land like vast orchards of malignant fruit... you can never renounce your citizenship there...

There are no metaphors powerful enough to describe the moment when you tell the children about the divorce.

*Divorces without children are minor-league divorces. To
look into the eyes of your children and to tell them that you
are changing all their tomorrows is an act of desperate
courage that I never want to repeat. It is also their parents'
last act of solidarity and the absolute sign that the
marriage is over.*

*The three girls entered the room and would not look at
me or Barbara. Their faces, all dark wings and grief and
human hurt, told me that they already knew. My betrayal of
these young sweet girls filled the room.*

*They wrote me notes of farewell, since it was I who was
moving out. When I read them, I did not see how I could
ever survive such excruciating pain. The notes said, "I love
you, Daddy. I will visit you." For months 1 would dream of
visiting my three daughters locked in a mental hospital. The
fear of damaged children was my most crippling
obsession...*

Certainly, I agree with this author that divorces without
children are minor-league divorces. But the damage to
children, it could be argued, takes place whether they are
living in a bad marriage or living with a divorce. However,
in answer to that, I want to tell you what one young man
confided in me.

"Shimshon," he said, "my parents' marriage was a
horror. But you know what we used to have nightmares
about?" I expected him to say, he had nightmares his
parents would hit each other. Or, that his friends would be
over when their parents started fighting. I was surprised.
"Our worst nightmare, the one that sent us scurrying into
each other's beds for comfort in the middle of the night,
was the fear that we'd have to choose between Mommy and
Daddy. How could we choose? We didn't care where we'd
actually live—children from bad marriages think very little
about their own wants, they have bigger problems—but we
were worried because if we chose Mommy, how could we

hurt Daddy like that? And if we chose Daddy, how could we face the pain in Mommy's eyes? What if we have to choose? There were four of us, so we'd sit and figure out how to divide ourselves up to cause minimal pain and rejection for either Mommy or Daddy, which two to Dad and which two to Mom."

If you fight but you leave the D-word out of it, at least your kids won't have fears of having to choose. I remember reading *Sophie's Choice,* a story about a Holocaust survivor who survived physically but her heart was killed by the Nazis. The most memorable scene from the book is where this mother who has a son and a daughter is forced by the Nazi officer to choose one child to live and take with her, and one to die in the gas chamber. She must choose or else he'll kill both, he tells her. So she chooses.

Agonizing isn't the word for such choices. And children do believe they would kill their parent if they chose the other, and parents often agree that this is so. "How could I live without you, *mamalle*?" they say. Oh, the guilt!

Don't let them think for a second that they might one day have to choose between Mommy and Daddy.

And if you really love those kids, for G-d's sake and for their sake and for your own sake, sit down and work things out. I'm telling you, you can! Be *frum* about it, be mature about it, be respectful and forgiving... you can.

If you don't, the loneliness may make you wish you had.

The unforeseeable loneliness is a killer. I had one woman call me up recently divorced, that she needs monetary help. So I went over to bring her money. It turns out she doesn't need the money. She just needed someone to talk to, but she didn't know how to ask for that.

Men don't have such a hard time getting remarried but women practically haven't got a chance. Especially with children.

35

So those kids you worked so hard to have and bring up… suddenly you're looking at them like a burden. If not for them, I might get remarried! You think the kids don't feel that?

Maybe we should return some of that stigma to divorce, like it used to be. Maybe simple shame would cause some people to work out their problems, or learn to live with someone with whom they don't have 55 things in common, but just a bunch of innocent kids who need both parents.

Nowadays everything is "no-fault" from car insurance to divorce. Even muggers blame their crimes on their addictions, which as we all now know are an illness and not their fault. So nothing is anybody's fault, so what's to be ashamed of?

Physical

The simple physical consequence of divorce is that both sides become very poor or if they were poor to begin with, poorer. Please, I don't have money to give you. C.S.S.Y. can't support everyone who decides divorce is a good option. And even if we could, do you want to live on charity? Do you realize you will have to struggle to pay the rent and the bills? Forget about nice clothes for all the dates you hope you'll get.

There are other physical problems with divorce, too, besides the financial ones. Simple, practical problems arise. Did you ever stop and think about your daughter's wedding? You cannot walk her to the *chupah* if you are divorced. The pictures will be a mishmash. Your kids' lives will be upside down, with them never knowing where they're going when and with whom and most of all, why. Why?

If you're considering getting a divorce, stop and check if your priorities are in order. I beg G-d to give me my health and *parnassah*, a healthy wife and healthy, happy children. These are important. I think people today have their values screwed up. In a divorce there are no gainers, no winners. No child ever benefited from a divorce (see exceptions below). If you're still looking for a divorce, stop and check if the values you have, and the things you want, are things the Aibershter meant for you to have, or are they things you learned in the movies or from T.V. or some magazine that should better be used to stuff up a mouse hole in the back hall.

A cancer has crept into the *frummer velt*—this epidemic of divorce. I never could define "incompatible" until I got to know people getting divorces. Now I can define it perfectly: "I don't have time to give this marriage a chance to work."

Don't tell me you fell out of love. I can't listen to such lunacy anymore! You love your child when he's good and when he's bad... you keep your mother when she acts nice and when she acts nasty... you forgive your father when he's warm and when he's aloof... you love the people you love, and you don't dump them just because divorce has become acceptable!

Don't expect a marriage counselor to solve your problems for you. Go home, lock the door, make a big pot of tea and get to work yourselves. If the marriage counselor advises you to split up, run, don't walk, out of his office! If he tells you there's no shame in divorce and you should consider it, get out of there fast before his lousy advice turns your kids into emotional cripples, G-d forbid. The kids will be okay if they see you argue once in a while, especially if you let them see you make up once in a while, too.

Don't look for a love story like in some trashy novel or some movie. Every *Yiddishe* home must write its own private love story. In this story you will find not roses and violins, but diapers and bills. But it can be, and should be, a love story nevertheless.

We all make mistakes so learn to forgive. Sometimes you can get so angry you just want to say... to say... *to say the D-word!!* But take a deep breath and count to ten. Once that word is spoken a certain innocence is gone forever. Before you say a word, you are master over it. Once you say it, it is master over you. You can't pull it back.

I read a statistic which I hope is not true—that 65% of children from divorced homes will also divorce eventually. If it's true I hope I'm retired from this business in 20 or 30 years when all the children from today's divorces grow up and get married. I don't want to be there, I don't want to see it, I want no part in it. I warned you. Here it is in print. Don't do it.

Loneliness

The loneliness you will experience if you divorce cannot be described in words on paper. It is a terrible, crushing burden. It becomes difficult to function, even at work. Children don't make up for it because they go to bed at 8 or 9 o'clock and you're left up all alone. G-d forbid if you take one of the older kids and start confiding in him/her; and using him/her as a surrogate spouse, as a confidante, or just for companionship; it is selfish and unfair and damaging.

How come our grandparents never got divorced? They were committed to working things out. Or were they more "compatible"? Did they have more money, easier lives? Were they not as smart as us?

And they had no marriage counselors and no psychologists either, just the Torah and *Shulchan Aruch*. But they knew one thing: Divorce means End, Finished, No Going Back, Alone, Lonely. This they didn't want; they figured that out in advance; they were pretty bright, our grandparents.

With the horrible proliferation of divorce in this country, lots of children's books have been written about it to help kids adjust. Those books are the saddest excuses for adults' selfishness that I have ever seen. One of them is supposedly written by a little girl about her "other-mother" and "other-father," in other words, her step-parents. She ends the book as follows: "Miss Burns once asked me how it feels to be a child with two families and I didn't know how to answer her. Now I think I do. I would probably say, 'It's complicated and sometimes I have problems, but mostly I feel just like anybody else.'"

Nothing could be further from the truth. The authors wrote it as they would like it to be. In truth a child going through the divorce of her parents feels totally cut off and different from her friends and classmates.

Conclusion

I would like to dedicate this article, and hopefully the good it will accomplish, to a dear and saintly rabbi, a man who worked with all his strength for *shalom bayis*, Rabbi Zalman Shimon Dvorkin, *zichrono l'vrachah*. He used to say, "Shimshon, the worst part of marriage is better than the best part of divorce."

Exceptions

I am purposely putting exceptions last, even after the conclusion, because I hope you won't get this far in the article. There are some exceptions where divorce should be chosen as an option.

Basically these fall into two categories. One is where the *halachah* says that a couple must divorce, *R"l*. It's not necessary to go into the reasons this might happen. And the second instance is when there is physical abuse, either wife abuse (beatings) or child abuse of any kind. If the man won't go for help and get himself better, it's better to get out because otherwise these sicknesses are carried down through the generations (abused kids grow up and abuse their kids).

And now, a *BRACHAH!* May G-d bless us and our families with health, wealth, and *shalom bayis* now and for generations to come. May the word *Gittin,* divorce, be only a *Gemara,* something to learn about in abstract.

Yours,
Shimshon

Chapter 9 - Help Your Wife

Tishrei 5750 – September 1989

The D-Word Hit Home

My article in the Shvat issue on divorce really seems to have hit a nerve. Many people have written letters about it and spoken about it and it was reprinted in the Australian *Jewish Women's Newsletter* (which hopefully the Australian Jewish men read too). This is good. If we open our eyes and read, and then open our minds and think, and then open our hearts and feel, then maybe finally we will open our mouths and talk to each other and work things out and stay married and show love and respect to each other. And consideration. Consideration is something that needs to be talked about.

Consideration

Sorry, fellas, this time you're going to get it. The ladies have gotten it from me plenty but this time you're in trouble.

You have to help at home.

Help, help, help. Help whenever you can, whatever you can. Your wife is not an Amazon. She is a person, and if she is nursing or pregnant then she needs even more help. She really could use more rest. Of course appreciation and moral support are imperative and there is no excuse for not giving at least that to your wife, but physical help is also necessary.

A True Story

Whenever I write that something is true, please believe me, it is. This man comes over to me and says that he wouldn't trust a non-Jewish cleaning lady to do Pesach cleaning. Plus it's a lot of money to hire one (which is the real reason?) BUT he doesn't have time to help clean. He expects his wife to do it all, with a houseful of kids too! I asked him to tell me what exactly he expects from his wife. Here's the list: 1) a clean house 2) delicious, homemade meals 3) a good mother to his children 4) she must look neat and pretty when he comes home from work!!!!! My friends, honestly, sometimes this particular man forgets to take out the garbage which is the bare minimum that men have always done even in the days before men did anything. In my opinion, "obnoxious" is too nice of a word for this man; he is disgusting.

Then and Now

Yes, guys, I know, when you were a kid your mother did all the housework and your father didn't do any. But, first of all, just because it once was that way doesn't mean it's right. Years ago when people were sick they used to be bled with leeches. Now we realize that isn't right! Well, maybe we should realize that just because Grandpa never helped Grandma, doesn't mean it was right!

And secondly, there's something else to consider here: Years ago, in your grandparents' and maybe parents' generation, roles were clearly defined. The women were completely in charge of the home and the children; the men were completely in charge of bringing in the money. The men didn't have to help at home because the women didn't have to go to work. Nowadays, however, many women are involved in activities outside the home, be it money-making activities or volunteer. This applies especially to the young couples on *shlichus* where the women do so much outside the home. Therefore, the men need to expand their roles and get busy inside the house too.

A third point to consider when yearning for "the way it used to be" is that we are having much larger families now than we had then. Maybe 50 years ago when the father didn't help, well, there were only four or five children to take care of. Now there are ten or 12, *kein yirbu.* With a really large family the father must *really* help out.

How?

Oh, please, I can't believe you asked that. How? I'll tell you how! Wash the kitchen floor. Vacuum the dining room. Diaper the baby. Bathe the children. Shampoo their hair (rub behind the ears). Wash the dishes (use steel wool on the frying pan). Easy-Off the oven. Wash out the garbage can when you change the bag. Carry the summer clothes down to the basement and carry the winter clothes up. Take the boys for haircuts. Take the girls for school supplies. Clean the chickens. Change the sheets. Clean up the *succah* after every meal. Take the kids to a park. Still need more ideas?

Her Worst Kid?

Your wife has plenty of children. From you she needs a grown man, not another child. Take a look around and ask yourself honestly, "Which one is my wife's worst kid?" If the answer is you, her husband, please change the way you act. Start simply by picking up after yourself. Then move on from there. Consideration and *mentschlichkeit* become habits after a while. Then when you see your children helping your wife and being considerate, you'll know it's because they're copying you! (Not *chas v'shalom* the other way—they see you ignore your wife when she needs help and so they do the same.)

Why Did This Happen?

I see so much immaturity in the husbands and I don't know where it comes from. Why does a man say to his wife, "No, darling, I will not do the Thursday night shopping. I will lie on the recliner and read the paper. Here are the car keys"??? Why? I have a little germ of a theory. Possibly, just theoretically, it all stems from those crucial years from age 18 'til 23. What are our young men doing during those important years, during the transition years when a boy goes from being a child to a married man? Unfortunately, many of our young men spend those five years doing... (you fill it in). Meanwhile, the girls are studying, working, earning money. learning the meaning of responsibility. Responsibility is the key word here. Many men learned laziness and self-indulgence while the women were learning responsibility.

Tishrei Reminder

I say it before Pesach, I say it before Tishrei. Don't spend money you haven't got. Don't bury yourself in debt. Don't look what other families have and try to have the same if you can't afford it. Don't run to a *gemach* for a luxury.

What, ladies, you thought I would leave you alone this time? No, I have something to say to you too. Help your husband so you can live within your means. No, I don't mean you should dump the kids somewhere and get a job. Someone has to raise them and you can do it like nobody else can because you're their mother. But I've already talked about this in previous issues. What I'm saying now is, help him by keeping expenses down. Don't keep up with the Joneses or the Yankel Todreses. Buy bargains and stretch food and clothing dollars. Don't waste. Nobody has to tell you how to watch the wallet, you know! Women are smart in that way. You alone can keep your husband out of debt.

Another True Story

My friend, Rabbi Zalman Shimon Dvorkin, *a"h*, told me this one. A young man came to him and said, "I work 10 hours a day to support my family. I come home at night and I relax for one hour and I learn for one hour. My wife wants me to help her with the kids. What should I do?" Rabbi Dvorkin answered, "Give up the hour of learning."

Now I never said you shouldn't learn in the evening! But what will the point of the learning be anyway? To have *ahavas Yisroel*, help another Jew. Even if that Jew is your wife.

Two Last Little Ideas

Wives: Do a little nice thing for your husband today. Put a warm note in his lunch bag. Or the night he works late set the table with stemware and candlelight for the two of you.

Husbands: The next time you have a Sunday off, pack sandwiches and take your wife and children on the Staten Island Ferry. It's fun and cheap.

Everyone: *I* know where Shimshon has to improve. *You* know where you have to improve, how you can make your marriage better and your family stronger.

So do it. Times are tough and every family needs strengthening, even or maybe especially yours.

With Love of One and All,
Shimshon

Chapter 10 - Common Sense

Kislev 5749 – December 1989

Everybody's got their *peckel tzores*.

Yup, absolutely everybody. The person you're jealous of... her house is fancy, her kitchen is Hollywood, her clothes are gorgeous, her kids are cute.... but did you know that she still has nightmares because of events she lived through as a child? That her life is nothing to be jealous of? It doesn't pay to be jealous of anyone because whether it's obvious or not, everybody's got their *peckel tzores,* their private burden. As a child I always had a secret desire: to wear a golden chain around my neck. But I knew my father would've killed me! (Now my son Benjy would probably kill me, may he live and be well until 120.) The other day a little boy saw the golden chain I do, finally, wear around my neck every day, and his eyes opened wide with envy. He really wanted a chain like mine. So I said to him, "May all anti-Semites wear a chain like mine!" because I wear it to alert people that I'm a diabetic. So don't judge people by what looks like a piece of jewelry. Maybe it's a sign of illness, and there you are, green with envy for it!

So let's start being satisfied with what we have instead of being jealous, instead of saying to ourselves, "So-and-So really has it good," or, "I wonder where they got the money for that."

Dennis Prager said it: The only people who don't have problems are people I don't know well.

Priority: A Happy Jewish Home

Instead let's concentrate on what's important, not what's doing by *yenem,* by the other guy. Rather, let's take a good look at what's doing by ourselves: Are we taking good care of our wives/husbands and children and grandchildren, making sure they have good love and a happy, comfortable place to come home to, someone warm and concerned to talk to?

In general I don't hold from psychologists and psychiatrists too much (more on this later), but I once heard one of them say on a radio talk show, "If your work life is miserable and your home life is fulfilling, you can still be a happy person. But if your home life is miserable, no matter how great things are at work you cannot be a happy person." Even that dumb radio person, and she was a psychiatrist *noch*, knew the truth. So instead of looking for an extra hour to squeeze in at work, we should be searching with all our might for one more minute to spend at home with the really important people in our lives.

Compassion

And once you realize that, and you start putting your own house in order, you may find you have a spare minute or a spare place at the table for someone less lucky than you, someone whose own parents didn't make sure he/she had a place to go and a listening ear, someone who is deathly lonely. In that case let your compassion show. In the *seforim* it says, if you bend over backward to help another person, in equal measure will G-d "bend over" to help you, undeserving though you may be. And in case you're wondering about someone, does he/she need my help? Or are they really quite alright without me? Here's a foolproof way to find out. Ask! NOBODY LIES OR JOKES ABOUT LONELINESS. This I am sure about from many years of experience with lonely people, *R"l*. When somebody says to you, "The worst part is the loneliness, I am so lonely," believe him; he is not lying or joking or exaggerating. Invite him over. There's an old song and I think these are some of the words (correct me if I'm wrong): "Consider yourself at home. Consider yourself part of the family. We haven't a lot to share—who cares? Whatever we've got we'll share." Or something like that, but you get the idea. Those few words, said to someone who is lonely, are the most beautiful words in the whole English language, or in any language.

What YOU Stand to Gain

YOU, my friend, and not the person you're helping, will be surprised. You'll be surprised to find that you have gained more than you gave away. I know a woman who was depressed. Although her husband made a nice living and was a nice guy, and her kids were healthy and doing well in school, she still found herself moping a lot. She wrote to the Rebbe for advice. The Rebbe told her to spend one hour each day in some sort of *tzedakah* work; visiting the sick, cooking for a *kimpitorin*, whatever. *Volunteering*, in other words.

If you're plagued by a general malaise, think about it for a second: Do you volunteer at all, for anything, ever? When was the last time? Maybe that's the elusive something that's missing from your life.

Read... Think... Act!

I know I sometimes repeat myself in these articles. But that's because I feel I'm writing about essential things, lifeblood issues. And it's not just for light reading… it's to make you think, and then to make you act!!! If three people pick up the phone to call three lonely people tonight, I'm glad I got writer's cramp over this thing. If one man or woman decides to go straight home to the *kinderlach* instead of stopping off for some *narishkeit* tonight, it was worth writing a whole article in the *N'shei Chabad Newsletter* for this. Like I've said before, we are a growing community. But let's be careful of what we are growing… hopefully flowers, not weeds; people, not wild animals. Which bring me to putting responsibility for the children where it belongs: on the home, not the school.

Improve Home. Don't Blame School

It's easy to pass the buck. But when it comes to our children, it's not getting us anywhere. Sure, the schools could be improved. Show me a school that cannot be improved, and I'll bring you breakfast in bed because you're dreaming. But those kids are our kids, not the school's kids. If your child grows up to be a *mentsch*, a light in the Jewish

47

world, a wonderful, kind, wise person, who will watch with tears in their eyes? The parents are the ones who watch such a thing with gratitude to G-d in their hearts and true love for their child. The teachers and principals and janitors and bus-drivers... well, they did their jobs well when the child was in their hands briefly, but it's not someone they're going to think about in 20 years. YOU, the parent, have a stake in how that child turns out. So grab hold of the finger you're busy pointing at the school, and bring the finger around 180 degrees until it's pointing at yourself. Yes, you! WE have to make our children and grandchildren into *mentschen*. WE are going to be watching in 20 and then 50 years, with G-d's help, and *shepping nachas* or G-d forbid the opposite.

A True Story

Honestly, this is true, and just as honestly, it hurts me to tell it. I was sitting at a bar mitzvah. A group of 13-year-old boys was outside throwing large rocks at passing cars and nearby homes and even passing people, causing damage, pain, and fear. One woman tried to stop the boys, but they answered her with unbelievable *chutzpah*. Sign of the times, I know. But the next day, the woman who had tried to stop the boys called up one mother and said, "You know your son was doing thus-and-thus..." And this is the part of the story that really eats me up. The mother answered, "Don't tell me. Call the principal."

Remember this: Nobody *sheps nachas* like you do when your children do well. And, G-d forbid, nobody will suffer like you will, if they should turn out not good. The principal won't suffer; the teachers won't take it personally; nobody will lose any sleep but you, the parent.

And, as I've said so many times in this *Newsletter* that you're probably bored of hearing it, the first step in becoming close with your kids, and having any influence over them, is to really listen to them with both ears, both eyes, and your whole heart and head, plus any other parts of you available, including your arms. Even 6-foot-tall children need a hug sometimes.

Crocodile Psychology

There was this fellow who used to kill crocodiles in Australia. After spending his entire life in the wilderness dealing with crocodiles and such, he came to Manhattan, to "civilization," to see the world. His friend took him to a party, and he heard some people talking about their "shrinks."

He asked his escort, "What do they mean, they're going to their shrinks?" So the friend tried to explain the idea of going to a psychiatrist or psychologist once a week, just to talk out your feelings, your problems, your past. The fellow listens intently, then says, "Oh, so in America you don't need 'mates!'" (Mates means friends in Australia.)

I'm not saying growing up, really growing all the way up, is easy. And I never said marriage was easy, either. You have to work at it, work at being a *mentsch* in your marriage, every day till 120. Your spouse is your best friend, and your mate (in Australian and American). And besides your spouse, you've got family and friends. Those are the best listening ears! It bugs me lately when I hear about people going to marriage counselors and all those professionals. Some couples go for five, ten years. I wonder, when are they ever pronounced "cured"? It's almost like you become married to the psychologist. They sure can take your money, if nothing else. A friend with a good set of ears, some patience, and a brain in working order could do better, I wager. And if you are thinking, "Oh, I wouldn't know what to say, I'd rather send my friend to a 'professional'..." here's my answer to that. Just imagine that it is your own child or brother or sister asking for advice. Then your answer will be the right one.

Before I send you off, I must add two more things about psychiatrists. First of all, a very dear friend once said, "I can't imagine any good coming out of a husband and wife being encouraged to say bad things about each other to a third person." That's a pretty fair assessment of some low-level marriage counseling. And the second thing is a joke. This guy goes to a psychiatrist and says, "I can't sleep! When I lie down on top of my bed, I'm sure there elephants underneath the bed. And when I go under the bed, I'm sure there are elephants on top of it! I just can't get any sleep—under, over, under, over, all night." The shrink nods wisely and says, "Come to me twice a week for six months at $50 a shot and I'll cure you." (All you math whizzes, come on, add it up—this cure is about to cost about two and a half thousand bucks.) The guy goes home. Months later, he meets the shrink at a party.

"Hey!" says the shrink. "How come you never came back?"

"My friend gave me some advice, and I was cured for $20. He advised me to saw the legs off my bed."

It's almost Chanukah as this is being written; I hope all of you light the little wicks together with family and good friends, not psychiatrists. I beg you all to forgive me if you were hurt by my mouth of my pen. I never meant any harm to any individual. I am to you what you are to me: a very dear and good friend.

A freilich Chanukah. Go easy on the *latkes*,
Shimshon

Chapter 11 - Life Is Tough

Tammuz 5750 – Summer 1990

The main point of my writing today is to tell you the story that I will tell at the end. Unfortunately, it is not a happy story, but, my friends, we all know that life has unhappiness in it, not just the major tragedies but all of life's smaller problems. Sometimes when a man struggles with *parnassah* day after day, week after week, month after month, year after year, he could use someone's wishing him *"Hamakom yenachem eschem,"* may G-d comfort you, although thank G-d everyone is alive. These small tragedies are sometimes harder to bear than the big ones. But, at least these smaller problems can be dealt with decently and kindly and maybe they can even be solved through decency and kindness.

Inviting Guests

For example, one problem some couples have is that one invites guests without consulting with the other and the quality or quantity of guests does not please the other. This is terrible and should not happen. If you must be a *"tzaddik"* or *"tzaddekes"* and invite a houseful of guests that your spouse can't handle, and you must watch him or her go off into the bedroom by himself/herself with a "headache," then I say this to you: *Shalom bayis* is more important than *hachnasas orchim*, and *ahavas Yisroel* means loving your spouse too! Make sure your spouse is comfortable with the guests before you say yes.

And once you do agree on the guests, and they're there in your home, remember that guests do not take priority. If you are the man, then what your wife says is more important for you to hear than what your V.I.P. guest says. If you're the woman, then when your husband speaks, do not get up and go into the kitchen to bring the soup. What he says is more important to you than getting soup to all the important guests. No-one is as important to you as your spouse.

The guests and the children will benefit indirectly if you have this attitude, because they will notice and learn— "H-m-m, this husband and wife really respect each other. Look how when one speaks the other pays careful attention." I read the papers every day and I read somewhere, "The most important thing a man can do for his children is to love their mother."

Two Suggestions

While we're talking about guests, here are two suggestions. First of all, if you usually have a heavy guest-load (as many Crown Heights families do), then once in a while (only you can say how often) make it a family-only Shabbos. You'll relax, you'll get to know one another a little more intimately, children included.

My second suggestion is, choose a family that you're close with, and switch off with them. One Shabbos lunch you go to them, one Shabbos lunch they come to you. Or do this with Yom Tov meals. You'll both save wear and tear, and provide each other with friendship and moral support besides.

Best Friends

But, again, whatever you do, only do it if both of you, husband and wife, agree and really want it. Don't please the neighbors. Don't please the kids. Don't please me! Please each other, that's your number one priority. Husband and wife must remember that they are each other's best friends when it comes right down to it. There's a book called *Welcome to the Real World!* by Wes Smith. It's full of commonsense advice.

"Eat good meals. Greasy burgers take their toll."

"No one sells a car because it runs too well."

But the advice I like the best out of the whole book is this:

"At some point in your life, your family will be all you have. Treat them right."

I would put the word "husband" or "wife" instead of family. Family can also be "too busy" or "can't afford it" or moved away or not answering the phone and the doorbell's broken. But your spouse will be there. And you'll need him or her. For sure. So be nice now.

Money Problems
One place where this is clearly seen (that husband and wife really only have each other to depend on) is in money matters. Your debts are not your mother's problem, or your brother-in-law's or your uncle's or even your best friend's who you've known since you were both two years old. The only person who shares those debts is your spouse. And the only one who can help you avoid getting into debt to begin with is Guess Who so confide in each other. Be honest and up-front. Wives, if you must run up a bill at a certain store, discuss it with your husband, preferably before you buy but certainly afterwards! Don't wait until the storekeeper calls your husband at work and your husband knows nothing about it and is humiliated by the storekeeper and furious at you. Husbands, if you are taking out loans to make ends meet, discuss these with your wife. Only she can help you cut expenses and repay the loans. You need her help badly, so turn to her. If she feels you are confiding in her as an equal and asking for help, she will give it. Contrary to myth, women can be great budget-keepers. Wives, I have given you lots of ideas for saving money in past articles so I won't repeat them. If you're a book person you may want to take out of the library *The Heart Has Its Own Reasons* by Mary Ann Cahill.

Only you can help your spouse in money problems. And in most other problems also. Share with each other, help each other.

There's a story that was told at one of the women's meetings before Shavuos. It has a beautiful lesson for all the couples out there who aren't considering divorce, G-d forbid, but they're not exactly happy with each other, either.

Back in the *shtiebel*, the Rav was the one everyone turned to, to solve every kind of problem. (The

53

psychiatrists hadn't taken over yet.) So this man goes to the Rav and says, "Listen, I have a terrible problem. I hate my wife! I know it sounds awful, but what should I do? She's nasty, she's a real witch, she cooks especially the foods I hate, the house is a wreck, she's a slob... I hate her! I want to kill her, but I know it's wrong to kill. What should I do?"

The wise Rav nods his head and looks into his *seforim*, then tells him, "There's a way to get rid of her without outright murdering her. It says here in the Medrash that he who makes a pledge to a *tzedakah* and does not pay it, his wife dies as a curse on him. So make a large pledge to *tzedakah* and don't pay it."

To this the man answers, "But I don't want people to know that I'm doing it purposely so my wife will die. People will wonder why I, such a poor Jew, am making such a big pledge!"

The Rav answers, "You're right. In order to mask your motive, just do one nice thing for your wife each day. Something small."

"Oh, no, Rabbi, I can't!" the man moans. "You don't understand! She makes me sick!"

"No, no," the Rav assures him, "I'm not telling you to be nice to her, after all. Just one small, deceptive thing a day. For example, today, compliment her on something at the table."

So the man goes and makes his pledge, and at supper, he says to his wife, "The bread tastes good tonight." She is shocked by this. But she decides to make sure and serve her husband only fresh, warm bread from now on, since he noticed and appreciated it. The next day he says something else nice. The third day he rocks the baby to sleep for his wife, etc. etc. You can guess the end already. By the time the pledge is due his wife has been responding to his cues and is treating him like a king. She's even been taking pains with her appearance to please him. Even the house is spic and span! He is panic-stricken and runs to the Rav.

"Rabbi!" he cries. "My pledge is due tomorrow and my wife will die and I love her! Life won't be worth living for me without her, the jewel of my life, my treasure, the center of the world as far as I'm concerned."

The Rabbi smiles and advises, "My son, you have no recourse now but to travel to the big city and borrow the money to pay the pledge."

And of course, the man spends the rest of his days repaying the loan to pay the pledge to *tzedakah* that he made in order to get rid of his wife.

Husbands, wives, just one kind word can set the wheel in motion, can start both of you off on the love affair you both want and deserve.

A Word About Children

Now that you are both treating each other with the love and respect that you both deserve, what about the kids?

I hear some parents complaining about the "noise" and the "mess" when their children bring home their friends. They should be like one mother of *ka"h* twelve, in our neighborhood, who says, "When my kids bring their friends here, I'm grateful. Where would I like them to hang out? Somewhere that I don't know what they're doing, who they're with, what they're talking about? Like this I can keep an eye on what's going on, who they're friends with." She realizes that noises and messes are not tragedies—estranged children are.

For all three of my children, my home was the center for all their friends. Many, many of them remember well the atmosphere here and how at home they felt. And Martha and I had the constant comfort of knowing exactly where our kids were, what they were doing, and, most importantly, with whom.

It's very important that your kids should have good friends. There's no question that your child will behave like his or her friends, definitely. And if there is a specific friend that your child "just can't" bring home—find out why

Make a cake for a friend of your child's. Be hospitable. The mess and the noise can be dealt with.

When our kids were growing up I remember there was one friend of theirs whose mother always said, "Don't bring your friends here, they give me a headache. And they track mud into the house." So they came here. But she lost her child. Don't lose your children over some mud on the tiles.

The Story

Now for the final story that's not a happy one. If you look up *The New York Post*, Friday, May 4, you can read the whole story yourself. A 29-year-old Jewish girl, Sue Laurie Rosenthal, a beautiful girl, died in the apartment of a very wealthy city official. She died from taking an alcoholic drink together with drugs.

The man didn't even give her a funeral. He wrapped her body in blankets and dumped it outside somewhere.

For him she gave her life.

I'm telling this because I know there are some married women out there, in their 30s and 40s, who wake up one morning in "mid-life crisis" or whatever the shrinks like to call it. They stand back and take a look at their lives and say, "Who needs this? I'm 42, I'm still young, but I'm gaining weight and these kids wear me down, and my husband is not exactly Mr. Romantic, and look at the fun that people *Out There* are having." Now by *Out There* she means in Hollywood, or in Manhattan, or heaven knows where, so long as it's out of Crown Heights or any *frum* community. Maybe she's reading too many trashy women's magazines about the lifestyles of the movie stars (who are the unhappiest lot of people in the world). If you ask me, even one of those magazines is one too many to read. She's thinking that if she were "skiing on the slopes" or "dancing at a party" or "wearing sequins" or "seen with a wealthy man" she'd then be happier than she is in her simple child-centered life that she has now at home with her man in Crown Heights.

What a mistake we make to think that way!

Our lives are a blessing. Being *frum* and married to someone who is faithful to you is a blessing. Do you think if you had Sue Laurie Rosenthal's companion, and his money and glittery lifestyle, you'd be happy? He wouldn't even give you a proper funeral after the drugs and alcohol did you in.

The article has a quote from Sue Laurie's mother that broke my heart.

"'She was an only child,' sobbed Rosenthal's mother, Ceil, who was sitting *shivah*—the Jewish practice of mourning for seven days—for her daughter."

I'll bet a million dollars for C.S.S.Y. that Mrs. Ceil Rosenthal would give her right arm that Sue Laurie should have had the chance, before she died such a terrible death and was dumped outside by the trash cans, to become a *baalas teshuvah*, marry a decent fellow, and have some children, and be busy doing mundane things like buying fruits and vegetables on Thursdays and picking up the little one at 1:00 and changing diapers in the middle of the night. Oh, for a "drab" existence like ours for Sue Laurie!

There is no better way of life. The truth is not in the magazines or movies but in Torah and *Shulchan Aruch*. Glamour is fleeting. A good life sustains you.

Letter to Mrs. Ceil Rosenthal

Dear Ceil Rosenthal,

My heart breaks for you that you will never have the pure joy of holding a grandchild, the child of Sue Laurie.

There are plenty of Jewish children and grandchildren who need mothers and grandmothers. My dear Ceil Rosenthal, come home. We need you here. Many families here would love to adopt you as a grandmother and you can do a world of good for them.

It would be a credit to Sue Laurie if you did. And maybe you could start lighting candles Friday night and Yom Tov, for you and for the soul of Sue Laurie.

Hamokom Yenachem Eschem...
Only G-d can comfort you...
Love, *Shimshon*

How lucky we are, all of us. We don't have the glitter and the glitz. Instead of high-heeled dancing shoes and sheer stockings our women wear flats and model coats. But we do know the meaning of happiness, if we'd only stop a minute and look. Look at Sue Laurie. Let's love each other, and ourselves.

In pain for all the pain in this world,
Shimshon

Chapter 12 - Jealousy and Forgiveness

Kislev 5751 – December 1991

In Respect

In sadness I begin this article with mention of Rabbi J.J. Hecht, may his soul rest in peace. You know how I'm always saying that people in this community need someone to talk to, a listening ear, someone to help them with their problems. But, people who can really do that job are so, so rare. J.J. was one who did it well—his advice was practical, what I call street-smart—and he did it 24 hours a day, seven days a week.

To know this all you had to do was see how many thousands of people came to the *shivah*. (May the family get together for only *simchas*.) J.J. didn't leave behind any fortunes or business empires, but be earned the respect of the world. He left over the *kesser shem tov*, the crown of a good name, which he earned with hard work, sincere hard work, over many decades. Only those who have gone to him for help, or those who know about all the help he gave people, can truly appreciate what a monumental loss this is. Maybe if about 200 people put in another hour a day helping people, we can try to begin to fill the role that he played here in Crown Heights. Where he got all those hours all by himself, nobody knows. He gave the credit to his wife, may she live and be well, Rebbetzin Chave Hecht. He said she always tried to take more on herself so he would be free to help people in trouble.

Bais Rivkah

When my daughter Chanie was six years old, we lived in East New York. Bais Rivkah, then as now the only Lubavitcher school for girls, was located on Stone Avenue in Brownsville. Rabbi Golden told me he couldn't send a bus just for Chanie. I wrote to the Rebbe and the Rebbe gave me permission to send her to a closer school in our own neighborhood, so long as it was a *frum* school. But I wrote back to the Rebbe that he should know that I wasn't going to do that... that I was going to let her go on the city buses with some of the worst elements, but she should go to Bais Rivkah, to his school.

That's why I can't stomach people sending their girls to non-Lubavitcher schools. If you're a Lubavitcher, support your school at the very least with your daughter's physical presence every day. This is the minimum you can do. If you're a Lubavitcher, you're not helping anyone else when you do this. You're helping yourself. If you don't build up the school, who should?

You're living here, you're actually facing the Rebbe every so often, and you're sending your daughter to another school? Tell me, would you come home to your mother, and in front of her face take the food she had prepared for you and throw it in the trash, and pull out your bag of take-out Chinese food? In front of her face? Well, you are doing just that when your daughter goes to a non-Lubavitcher school.

What's coming next is not some kind of curse or threat. It is simply the kind of knowledge that comes with watching what happens over six decades of life. It has been said not just by me but by many older people in the community who have seen many generations grow up, and how they turn out. And here it is. Lubavitchers who take their children out of Lubavitcher schools and send them elsewhere are often sorry later. Eventually these parents pay a price for their decision. So do not make a decision like that hastily, or for small reasons.

Jealousy

Now that I got that off my chest, about Bais Rivkah, I can get down to what I really wanted to talk about this time. The problem of jealousy. Some people call it "keeping up with the Joneses." The kind of jealousy I'm talking about is always related to physical pleasures and treasures, never to spiritual. To be jealous of Torah learning or more kind acts is good! In physical accomplishments like nice kitchens or fancy clothes we're supposed to look at those who have less than us; in spiritual accomplishments like visiting the sick or inviting lonely people in, we're supposed to compare ourselves to those who have more than us. (I know you're surprised what a *talmid chacham* I am.)

Jealousy (of the wrong sort) is so harmful to normal life that there's a prayer in *Shemoneh Esrei* to please spare us from feelings of jealousy.

The Tenth Commandment

My dear friends, if you know me you know I am no rabbi and not a person who is critical and full of *mussar.* Anything I write or say, I am speaking to myself also.

The tenth commandment is: Do not covet your neighbor's house, wife, etc. To covet someone's house or fancy car will only lead to unhappiness. Even if you do manage to acquire what they have, they're so rich they'll soon move out and then you'll have new neighbors and who knows what kind of kitchen *they'll* build? No, it's much better for your health and your marriage and your finances and everything to kick the jealousy habit right from the start. Don't look at them, it's not your business and don't ask how much this or that costs in someone else's house. What's the difference to you? When you'll need it and be ready to buy it you'll get the *Consumer Report* and find out the prices. Don't ask ahead of time.

Spouse Jealousy: The Worst

Coveting your neighbor's house isn't the worst problem. The very worst, the most harmful kind of coveting that I know of, is when someone covets the treatment someone else's spouse gives him.

A man walks into his neighbor's house at 7:00 and sees how his neighbor's wife is setting down before her husband a hot steaming dish of roast beef and potatoes, with a fresh salad on the table. Not only that, but while she is serving him she is smiling sweetly, and the children are already bathed. He goes home in one unbelievably lousy mood and immediately starts picking on his wife. "These kids stink," he snarls, picking at his tuna sandwich. His wife turns away with a hurt look on her face. "You're right, they need baths. Can you help me?" She is pregnant and cannot bend over the tub easily. He sighs. He sits there eating his cold sandwich and he is not happy with his lot.

Does he know all the facts? No one ever does. No one really knows what goes on between husband and wife, except for that husband and wife. What looks good could be bad. What looks bad could be good.

For example, that neighbor's wife who was dishing up the roast beet—well maybe her husband's doctor called her just that day to tell her that her husband's cholesterol was dangerously high and he must cut out all meat and fat. So the first thing Mrs. Perfect does is buy the fattiest roast beef she can find and make it for him with tons of gravy. This is love? This is what you're jealous of? And maybe your wife made tuna sandwiches tonight because two weeks ago you both sat down and agreed on a food budget and she is conscientiously, like a good loving supportive wife, trying to stick to it. She found a crazy sale on tuna and stocked up. Nu? Why covet?

Pointing Out Other's Talents Doesn't Help

Maybe some husbands and wives think, if they just point out all the shining examples around, their own spouses will automatically improve. Just the opposite happens.

A friend of ours, a middle-aged woman, still remembers with pain how when she was small her mother used to tell her to look at her cousins. These particular cousins knew how to sew, dance, sing, and cook, and were terribly polite to their elders besides. Do you know, this woman could never bring herself to pick up a sewing needle. The comparison had hurt her too much.

If you want your wife to serve you a beautiful dinner, try this: "Honey, I really love when you make [name your favorite]. You make it like nobody else! I feel so good when I come home to a great dinner like that." Guaranteed, you will get more delicious dinners, and with a smile, too. But try this: "Listen here, Wife. I went next door the other night and what do you think I saw? Mrs. Perfect was serving her husband roast beef, potatoes, the whole works. And, the children were all bathed already. Why can't you ever do that?" Guaranteed, you will have one unhappy wife and very few dinners to come home to. Comparisons just hurt too much. They never help.

Wives, You're Not Off the Hook!

Sorry, wives, but you're often just as guilty. Women are notorious husband-comparers.

Many a woman greets her husband with these words, "You should have seen what I saw today at the neighbor's house. Why, her husband was down on the floor scrubbing the kitchen floor. And it was only 5:00. And he had two kids on his back while he did it." Wait! What do you know about the real story? Maybe this guy is on the kitchen floor because he's too damn lazy to stand up. He's been washing that floor all day. And maybe he refuses to go out and get a job, and she's *platzing* inside because he's home all day.

Appreciate

The bottom line is, stop looking at what's doing by *yenem* and concentrate on the good points of your spouse, and appreciate. If things need to be changed, work on it in a kind and loving and smart way and not by comparing your spouse to Mister or Mr. Perfect down the block. Believe me, it's not so perfect there as it looks.

Living Examples: All Parents

You may not feel like changing the way you act, even if you know in your heart of hearts that it's really not so good. But how are you going to feel when in ten or 20 years, you have to sit back and watch your grown children behaving just like you're doing today? Because you can count on it happening.

There's one thing that's never a waste of time, and that is spending time talking with your children. Talk about responsibility. Make sure they each have a job in the house; they should feel like they're part of the family in this way. And make sure you know what's going on with them, who their friends are, where they're going. And make sure they feel loved. The furniture won't be there in 30 years, the kids will. Invest in what's real and lasting, the kids.

A Cure for Jealousy

Maybe someone out there is reading this and thinking, "I know jealousy is terrible but I just can't help it, I'm a terribly jealous person." Well, here is a suggestion for you that will definitely cure you. Volunteer to spend some time helping out at a nursing home, or in the pediatric ward of the hospital. If that's too tough for you, how about a couple of days right here helping out with Chevra Simchas Shabbos v'Yomtov. After you see some of the *tzoros* that come through here you won't be jealous ever again. People who are desperately poor, desperately sick, desperately lonely. The one thing they all have in common is their desperation, the utter urgency of their need, whatever it may be. This past Motzoei Rosh Hashanah was 13 years since the Rebbe, *shlita,* made us into an organization. My kids and their friends still remember when we used to pack up boxes of food Thursday nights and Benjy would deliver them all over Crown Heights. We've grown since then at an incredible pace, but believe me I pray to G-d we should go out of business.

Forgive and Forget

I met a woman last summer who told me her complaints against her husband. She wasn't lying, every complaint was true. But what was terrible here was that she wasn't even trying to forgive him, and to concentrate on the good points of which her husband had many, believe me. I never saw a man so involved with his teenage sons, setting an example for them, taking them to shul, learning with them, etc.

Many women would give their right arm for their husbands to be such good fathers. But anyhow, she had her complaints. And she carried *The List* in her mind wherever she went, whoever she spoke to. She always knew, at a second's notice, what his sins had been, and as the years went by she always kept adding to *The List*. He was like a condemned man. He didn't stand a chance. Whatever he sinned once was always held against him.

How much sweeter is life together if two people can forgive and forget. Forget! Would you really want your spouse to keep *The List* of all your past transgressions? Haven't you had your difficult times when you've been a royal pain to live with? Forgive, and then forget. You're going to be together, you might as well maximize the chances for friendship and liking between you. Forgetting is important. If you're the keeper of *The List*, tear it up and throw it out. If your spouse is, show him/her this article.

Speaking of Forgiveness

This article never made it into the Tishrei issue so I didn't get a chance to say, before Yom Kippur, that I ask everyone to forgive me if I have ever hurt or embarrassed you in any way. If I did it, it was not intentional because I love you. May G-d bless you with your needs, physical and spiritual. And may our dear Rebbe, *shlita*, be healthy and blessed with everything he wants and needs. We surely need him.

Love,
Shimshon

Chapter 13 - A Friend in Need Is a Friend Indeed

Shvat 5752 – February 1992

Please, be well!

Now, you're thinking: not only does Shimshon fancy himself a speaker, a *shadchan*, a family man, and a writer... now he's also becoming a health expert!

All I want to say about health is that we must guard ours. The Torah says we have to and common sense agrees. Smoking is no good, makes too many fights between husbands and wives, besides (and because), it's very unhealthy. And with food—did you know that the healthiest foods are also the cheapest? You know I'm always trying to convince people to live within their means, to spend sensibly, not to get into debt for non-essentials. High-fat usually means high price. You be smart now, while you're young, before you have to give up steaks and 7-layer cake on doctor's orders. Train the kids to eat healthy. Look around at most people in their 60's, 70's, 80's, —you'll see! The ones who are still alive and healthy and vigorous and independent are the ones who learned to control their eating years before.

My Friend's Grandmother, *ka''h*

A friend of mine has a grandmother who at 82 takes brisk walks once a day in her lavender-colored walking shoes. This elderly woman, G-d bless her, she should live until 180 and have *nachas* from her children, grandchildren and great-grandchildren, didn't start eating healthy yesterday. In her 50's yet, which was when she arrived in this country, she was cooking vegetables and making hot cereal every morning. No fried eggs for her. And now look at her, reaping the rewards. My friend is rightfully proud of his grandmother.

And don't forget to ask Hashem for good health because no matter what you eat or don't eat, exercise or don't exercise, stress or no stress, it's all in His hands. Yes, He wants us to do whatever is in our power... but then it's up to Him.

And if you won't eat healthy because it's healthy, then do it because it's cheaper. I always beg of you, my friends, to live within your means. Debts and money problems cause more tension between husband and wife than any other problem.

Be Happy This Purim

Another way to be smart—and a good person, too—with money is to give the money you would spend on fancy *shalach manos* to Chevra Simchas Shabbos V'Yom Tov. You know how you feel about all those pineapples and cupcakes at the end of Purim? Well, that's how the people you send them to feel, too.

On the other hand, do you know how it feels to be a father of 12 and just laid off from your job? About to lose your house? Very not good. And how does it feel when C.S.S.Y. comes in and gives a hand? Well, that's how you spell R-E-L-I-E-F. So take that pineapple and cupcake money, say about $300 or $400 per Purim? —and send a check to C.S.S.Y., 593 Montgomery Street, Brooklyn NY 11225. There are so many people in such terrible need, you wouldn't believe it unless you came and sat in my house for a day. Then you'd see the desperate souls who knock at the door and come in asking for help, outright asking. I can't help them unless you help them. And when I come around in 770 with my big bucket, please throw in a $20, not a single. We've got big families who need big help. Marrying off their children, late with their mortgages, all kinds of pressures, and all kinds of *tzoros*. When you see me coming, open your wallet, take out a dollar, and give me the rest.

Talking in the Car

Remember I once told you to take your wife and go for a ride? If you live in Boro Park, go for a ride in Crown Heights. If you live in Crown Heights, go for a ride in Boro Park. If you live in Canarsie, go for a ride in Manhattan. You get the idea. Just get out and go. Well, now I would like to go into a little more detail about those rides. On your next one, please bring up the subject of *shalach manos*. Discuss it between the two of you, and decide if you'd feel better sending the money to C.S.S.Y. for people who really need the food. And you can get lots more for your food dollar when you're buying cereals and carrots and potatoes, than when you're buying chocolates and baskets and fancy red paper.

So, yes, you should be happy this Purim, and make other people happy, too.

Everyone Can Give

There are so many people who need help in this neighborhood, in this state, in this world. The only way everyone will be helped is if everyone also helps. In one way you might be a taker, someone who needs help, but in some other way you can give too. No matter how needy you yourself are, you can also give. You can help someone else. Somebody who comes to me for help a lot was feeling sorry for himself once. He told me how sick he is. Does he think Martha and I are in perfect health?! But I listened on. Then he told me about his money worries. About his job that's shaky. His marriage. Kids. How many people wish they had a marriage and kids to be concerned with? Finally I told him that he had to solve his problems, yes, but he also had to find a few minutes to help someone else sometimes. He sighed and said, "I have nothing to give someone else."

Here is my suggestion to him and people like him who think that because they don't have a lot of money, or perfect health, or some other optimal condition, that they have nothing to give.

The next time some pathetic *nudnik* calls you on the phone and starts to get his problems off his chest, don't cut him off with a curt, "Listen, I gotta go now, good luck, bye." Instead, give him the time of day. Take out an extra five minutes and listen quietly as he unloads his burden. Your burden will still be there after you hang up. But his will feel lighter because he was allowed to share it with you.

No matter how bad off you are, you have five minutes on the other guy's phone bill, don't you?

What Is a Friend?

We are not a fish. Don't sit there with your mouth open like that, trying to figure out the connection between the other guy's phone bill and **What Is a Friend**. There's no connection. This is my article and I can skip around between topics if I feel like it. And right now I feel like it.

First, what a friend is not. A friend is not someone who says, when you tell him about a *shidduch* which was spoken to you, "I just can't see you two together." Or, "You deserve better than that." With friends like that, who needs enemies? A true friend will say, *try it. Go out together. The boy is healthy, normal, kind, works and makes a living. So go.*

A friend is happy with you in good times and willing to lend a real hand, not just an ear, when things are not so good. I know someone here in Crown Heights with a very large family, *ka"h*. She told me that because she has lots of relatives in Crown Heights, she doesn't receive help after she has a baby because everyone assumes someone else is taking care of her. Not one to sit around feeling sorry for herself, however, this woman does whatever she can in advance to make things easier for herself, cooking and freezing ahead and arranging babysitters to help with the other kids, etc. Well, one time, a few days after she gave birth the doorbell rang and a neighbor named Malka, a woman who she had chatted with at the bus stop in the mornings but no more, came in with an aluminum foil pan. In it were a few pieces of fried fish, some green beans, and some noodles. The neighbor said, "I wouldn't even begin to know how much to prepare for a family the size of yours, but here is at least a hot lunch for you, the *kimpitorin*."

Do you know that when this woman tells this story, her eyes fill with tears. She is so touched that this Malka brought over this lunch for her, when everyone else says, "Oh, she has so many relatives," or, "They have money, they can buy ready-made food." Although they don't really know each other very well, still, this woman considers Malka a real friend and always will think of her this way.

A friend is someone who tells you the advice he would give his own child, whether it's about a job or a house or whatever.

A friend advises you to take it easy with big spending until you can afford it.

A friend tells you privately when the house is dirty or the kids aren't dressed right, and shows you how to fix those things! Yes, they are important. More on cleanliness later.

A friend ALWAYS tells you good things about your own spouse, and NEVER badmouths your spouse to you. Notice, I said ALWAYS and NEVER because these are cardinal rules! All it takes is a shrug, a face, and the marriage turns sour. Or, on the other hand, an appreciative smile, a kind word, and it's saved. Here's how it works.

Sally tells Bertha, "My Joe, he's such a pain. I asked him three times to take out the garbage. Finally, I just did it myself, with my bad back."

Now Bertha is holding the world in her hands. If she is a good friend, she will chuckle and say, "He must have had his mind on something from work. He works long hours, but you always told me how generous he is with you and the kids. A nice guy, your Joe."

Or if she is not a real friend, she'll roll her eyes heavenward and sigh, "That's incredibly insensitive, you know? I mean, he knows about your bad back, doesn't he? There's no way he could not know. How can you excuse a thing like that?"

Cleanliness: It Counts

Some people have a hard time with keeping the house and the people in it clean. Maybe they weren't raised with such large families so it's overwhelming. Or maybe they just don't know how or how often to bathe the kids or wash their clothes. Believe me, if you are a real friend, here's the true test. *Show* your friend how to improve the situation.

I know of a woman out on *shlichus* in California. She has a lot of children and very little money. But you would never guess from looking at those children. She buys their clothing in thrift shops for literally pennies ($1.25 for a child's sweater) but she takes it home, washes it well, irons it and sews on an appliqué or a little bow. Then she wraps it in tissue paper and presents it her child. And she is careful about hems and stains and shoe polishing. What a wonderful thing, to be so thrifty and clean and tidy. And this on a *shliach*'s salary.

Real Help Is Hands-On

If you have a friend whose house is really a disaster, don't talk about her to your other friends. Don't pipe up, "You can't imagine what the inside of her house looks like."

You'll enlarge their imagination some other way, maybe they could look at clouds through your skylight some time. For now, go over to your friend privately and say, "Look, I'd like to help you with your house. When can I come, and where shall we start?" Or mention that kids need to be bathed more than once a week, and their nails cut. *Go over and do it.*

Go ahead, do it! If you come to her out of an honest desire to help, and speak warmly and sincerely, and don't embarrass her, she will appreciate it beyond all words.

Married Couples, I'm Talking to You

And the best friend you have is your spouse. Treasure your husband, treasure your wife, he/she is there for you and wants you to be happy. Everything I said about being willing to get up and help goes double and triple when it's your own spouse in need. This is true whether it's the husband who wants his phone messages taken accurately, or it's the wife who wants a hand with the kids' bedtime.

Appreciate each other. Did you ever see an old couple, a really old couple, where both partners are in their 80's or 90's? All Jews should only live to enjoy such a blessing. Do you think that old couple wastes time fighting? Do you think they bicker about who said what, when? They appreciate every day, every night, every moment they have together. They know that too soon it may be over.

Well, time flies for the rest of us too. We live in a jet age, people get sick fast, people lose their jobs fast, before you know it you're in trouble or, hopefully, out of it. So don't waste time fighting.

When I talk to you I am also talking to myself and my own children. Let's be good to each other.

And please don't forget to give to C.S.S.Y. before Purim and all the time.

Life is tough so hang on... till next time,
Shimshon

Chapter 14 - Tough Times Require Strong Actions

Kislev 5753 – December 1992

It is very upsetting and sad and devastating to us all that the Rebbe is not involved in helping us through our daily problems like he used to be. May Hashem grant him a miraculous *refuah shelaimah* very quickly. But it seems that with the Rebbe sick, *R"l*, the whole community is sick. More marriages are in trouble than ever before. Maybe because the Rebbe's answers and letters and dollars and face-to face encouragement held many faltering marriages together. Maybe because when the mood is down, the *yetzer hara* has the perfect landing ground. Where there is happiness the *yetzer hara* can only hover ineffectually overhead, but he can't land anywhere.

My friends, let's not be hopeless. We have to do more for ourselves now. We have to take upon ourselves more friendliness, more love, more good sense (it's so uncommon, that I can't call it common sense). This friendliness has to be shown, first of all, between husband and wife. And then, between neighbors, relatives, friends (or former friends), and EVEN (OR ESPECIALLY!) BETWEEN ENEMIES.

The Ugliest Issue

The ugliest thing I ever had to talk about is divorce. It's so full of pain and anguish, and especially the pain of innocent, scared children is so terrible to see. When those children come to me for affection, I know their parents are too involved in World War III to hug those kids (in a way that feels real to the kids).

I already wrote about it at length in a previous issue. Although I'd like to reprint it, I'm not the editor. So let me just say, again, in summary, that you young women who think you'll improve your lives with divorce, believe me, it'll only get worse. If you stay single after the divorce, you'll be a single divorced mother with children to take care of. Ask one of them how it feels. If you remarry, I can swear to you in print in this *Newsletter* that the only man who will ever love your kids like a father is their own father. To every other man, they are nuisances, pests, an obstacle to the marriage (not an enhancement of it), a financial drain, and a marital strain.

Better, much better, to work on the marriage you already have, where the kids are happy and loved by both parents. If somebody is tempting you with how wonderful your life will become if you get that divorce, don't believe them! That person is the *yetzer hara* in flesh and blood. And whom will you hurt the most? Your own sweet, innocent children.

It's Contagious!!

Over the years, listening to people's problems, I have noticed a terrible phenomenon, and also a wonderful phenomenon. The terrible phenomenon is that divorce seems to be contagious among friends. First one woman decides she want out of a marriage, then the next thing you know, her best friend follows her example and before you know it there are three friends in on the deal, planning the good times they'll have once they get rid of their husbands, G-d forbid. They don't know the misery they're in for, and their kids are in for.

You see how important it is to pick the right friends, friends who influence you for the good??!!

Because then there's the other side of the coin, the wonderful phenomenon. I know of a woman who wanted a divorce. She just didn't want to struggle with her husband anymore, he was too difficult to live with, not good with the kids, nothing. She became friends with another woman, who, like everyone, has her share of problems but doesn't let the D-word come out of her mouth when she's talking to her husband. Whatever comes up, she is determined to work it out or learn to live with it. She knows there's no *groiseh glicken* waiting for her out there, so she's happy with the qualities her husband does have. Well, when the first woman became friends with the second woman, she too adopted this attitude. She, too, tried to concentrate on her husband's good qualities, thank him for them, and stop focusing on his faults. She absorbed her friend's attitude that "the alternative stinks" so let's work on what we've got. And now it's been months and I no longer hear her asking for a divorce. She is working things out to the best of her and her husband's ability. She's not thrilled with things (yet), but I'll tell you this: her kids are turning out okay. And they'll always have their parents' home to return to, and it will be a good home, a peaceful haven for them. And they are learning by seeing, that we can work out our problems, not run away from them and be selfish about them.

Enough about this. On to children. Spock, Stock, what's the difference?

Show Your Kids You Care

I get upset sometimes when I see a guy walking to shul and his kids are ten steps behind him, trying to catch up. He's rushing ahead, deep in thought, *fartracht* about goodness only knows what. Listen, Tatty, you have to walk to shul anyway, right? So utilize the time to hear what's on your child's mind, to impart values by giving your opinion on it. Don't waste the time. Another year or five or ten, and that kid won't walk with you and talk with you if you pay him, unless you've done it with him since he's small. Show him you're really interested in what's on his mind. Listen carefully to what he says. You're his father. You're her mother. Now is the time, when they're small, when they're home. You can't become close with your kids starting when they're 18. If you start at 18 months, you're still slightly late, but you've got a chance. The best is if you start at 18 seconds. Then they really need you, they want you, they're open to whatever you say.

Don't Be Afraid to Cuddle Up

Don't run so fast to the psychologists. Listen to me, I'm telling you, I see the result of all the psychologists' advice, and they're not so good. First try it my way, maybe it'll work. Cuddle up with your kids. Let the kids into your room, especially when they're scared at night.

To need and want human closeness is, well, only human.

Sometimes people of all ages just want to be near people who love them. No words, no counseling, no advice, just "be there," be together, be available, simply sit there.

Sometimes the tiniest babies are forced to sleep alone. It's only in this century, in our developed Western culture which has allowed us to afford all these separate bedrooms and separate beds for each child, that it has become "good." It's neither good nor natural. Alone becomes lonely all too fast.

There are some old people, who have long since lost their spouses, who will break into tears if somebody puts an arm around them. They are so touch-starved that they cry. Is there anybody like that in your family? If so, don't be stingy with the hugs. And as for your children, cuddle up— it's fun.

Kids and Housework

I'm happy that people are getting help in the house. Why should a woman work her fingers to the bone if there's an option? But I'm not happy to see some kids growing up like little princes and princesses, never having washed a dish, not even making their own beds or picking up their dirty laundry off the bathroom floor.

Every child is a member of the household, and should be not just a parasite but a contributing member of the household. Don't let them get away with not helping. If you do, you're hurting the kid in the long run.

Besides teaching the kid responsibility and giving him the skill and abilities he/she will need as an adult… you're also showing them that *ahavas Yisroel* means your own mother, too.

Remember, we have to be strong now. I'm talking to you and my children and myself too. Let's love each other, and really help when help is needed.

Love,
Shimshon

All the articles in this book are reprinted from the *N'shei Chabad Newsletter*, a periodical which is issued five times a year from Brooklyn, New York. To subscribe or to purchase back issues, please visit www.nsheichabadnewsletter.com.

Glossary

a"h - alav or aleha hashalom, may his/her soul rest in peace

Aibershter - G-d

ahavas Yisroel - love for a fellow Jew

baruch Hashem - thank G-d

basherte - predestined spouse

baalei teshuvah - people who returned to a Torah-observant lifestyle

B.T.'s – short for baalei teshuvah

brachah - blessing

bris - circumcision

bubby - grandmother

chassidishe kinder – Jewish and Hasidic children

Chassidus - philosophical understanding of Judaism

chas v'shalom - G-d forbid

cheder rebbi - male teacher in Jewish school for small children

chossid - follower of the Rebbe

chupah - marriage ceremony

chutzpah - nerve, gall

fartracht - deep in thought

frum - Torah-observant

frumkeit - religious lifestyle

frummer velt - Torah-observant world

gemach - interest-free loan society

Gemara - Talmud

goyim - gentiles

groiseh glicken - great good luck

halachah - Jewish law

hachnasas orchim - hosting guests

hanhalah - faculty

Hashem - G-d

ka"h - short for kein ayin hara, may the evil eye do no harm

kein yirbu - may their numbers increase

kimpitorin - a woman recovering from childbirth

kinderlach -children

krechts - sigh
l'havdil - to keep separate
lashon hara - saying bad things about others
lechatchilah - to begin with
mashpia, mashpiim (plural) - wise friend(s), mentor(s)
maaser - a tenth of one's earnings, referring to the Biblical obligation to give a tenth to charity
Medrash - stories from the Torah
Megillah - the story of Purim
mentsch - a decent, mannerly person
mentschlichkeit - decency, good manners
midos tovos - good qualities
mishugass - craziness
mitzvah - commandment, good deed
mosdos - organizations
mussar - criticism, toughlove
nachas - mix of pride and joy
narishkeit - nonsense
noch - to add to the irony
nosh - snacks
nudnik - a person who is a pain in the neck to others
parnassah - livelihood
peckel tzores - challenges or difficulties
platzing - feeling frustrated to the point of explosion
p'shat - simple meaning
R"l - Rachmana litzlan, may the Merciful One come to his aid
refuah shelaimah - complete recovery
seforim - Jewish books
shadchanim - matchmakers
shaitel - wig married women wear to cover their hair
shadchan - matchmaker
shalach manos - food gifts for Purim
shalom bayis - peace at home or peace between spouses
shidduch, shidduchim (plural) - marital match(es), or one's actual fiance or fiancee

shlita - may he have a good, long life
shliach - someone acting as his emissary or agent of the Rebbe
shlichus - a mission one is doing on behalf of the Rebbe
Shemoneh Esrei - major prayer
shepping nachas - taking pride and enjoyment
shomer Shabbos - keeps Shabbos
shtiebel - small village or small shul
shul - synagogue
Shulchan Aruch - Jewish law
simchas - happy occasions
succah - wooden hut where we eat on the holiday of Succos
talmid chacham - scholar, knowledgeable and wise person
Tatty - Daddy
tzaddik / tzaddekes - righteous person with no sins
tzedakah - similar to charity, but we are obligated to give it (it's not optional) so it's from the root of righteousness; it's only right
tzores - challenges or difficulties
yenem - the other guy
yeshivos - religious schools
yetzer hara - evil inclination
Yiddishe - Jewish
Yiddishe nachas - Jewish pride and joy
zaide - grandfather
zichrono l'vrachah - of blessed memory